The Craft of Language and Literary Research

Syed Mohammed Haseebuddin Quadri

ATLANTIC
PUBLISHERS & DISTRIBUTORS (P) LTD

Published by
ATLANTIC
PUBLISHERS & DISTRIBUTORS (P) LTD
7/22, Ansari Road, Darya Ganj,
New Delhi-110002
Phones : +91-11-40775252, 23273880, 23275880, 23280451
Fax : +91-11-23285873
Web : www.atlanticbooks.com
E-mail : orders@atlanticbooks.com

Branch Office
5, Nallathambi Street, Wallajah Road,
Chennai-600002
Phones : +91-44-48531784, 28411383
E-mail : chennai@atlanticbooks.com

Printed in India at Nice Printing Press, A-33/3A, Site-IV,
Industrial Area, Sahibabad, Ghaziabad, U.P.

Bismillah ar Rahmaan ar Raheem
Ya Mohammed Mustafa Sallallahu Alaihi Wa Aalehi Wa Sallam

For
My father and master,
Dr Syed Mohammed Hameeduddin Sharafi

Acknowledgements

First, I thank Lord Almighty Allah and His Beloved Messenger Holy Majesty Mohammed Mustafa (*Sallallahu Alaihi Wa Aalehi Wa Sallam*) for bestowing Grace on me so that I could author this book.

I am thankful to my father Dr Syed Mohammed Hameeduddin Sharafi for all his guidance, and in whose company spending just a day is enough to become a true scholar. I am also grateful to my mother whose appreciation always makes me go for big things in life. I do not have words to express my gratitude to my wife whose only aim of life seems to be my happiness. I thank my children whose company makes me forget everything; and my brothers—Dr Mufti Syed Saifuddin Quadri Hakem Hameedi, Dr Syed Raziuddin Quadri Hassan Hameedi, and my sisters who always appreciate whatever I do.

My acknowledgements are also due to all those scholars and publishers whose works I enlisted in bibliography and whose contributions I drew upon in this book profusely.

For their direct or indirect encouragement that helped me complete this project, I thank Professor Amina Kishore, Professor Wahab Qaiser, Professor T.V. Kattimani, Professor Khalid Sayeed, Professor Shaikh Mohammed Rahmathullah, Dr Mohammed Abdul Azeem, Mr Mohammed Abdul Muqsit Khan, Dr Shugufta Shaheen, Dr Gulfishaan Habeeb, Mr S. Omprakash, Mr G. Govind, Dr Mir Shujaath Ali, Dr Abbas Khan, Dr Badiuddin Ahmed, Mr Syed Khaja Safiullah, Mr Zia-ul-Haq, Mr Zainul Abedeen, Dr Karan Singh, Dr Ratnakar, Mr Seshu Babu, Mr Ghouse Pasha, Mr Chandrashekar, Mr Bhaskar, and Mr Shaik Mohammed Shafiullah.

Syed Mohammed Haseebuddin Quadri

Preface

Research is enquiry, method is system and thesis is a style of communication. This statement ensues that research is an effort, method is its systematization and thesis is its recorded manifestation. Thus, any book on research in reality becomes the presentation of recorded manifestation of effort systematization. Research method and thesis involve the concepts of contribution, system, and dissemination respectively.

As a teacher when I took up 'research methodology' to teach the class of MPhil—the lead-in course to doctoral research—I started gathering material, which besides the guides comprised my own experiences as research scholar.

However, very soon I realized that with the interminable expansion of knowledge and the accessibility to unlimited sources of information with just a click of a computer key, teaching research methodology now is equivalent to carrying out a groundbreaking research itself. The participants in MPhil and PhD programmes do not require teaching of research methodology, rather they require 'training in research methodology', for the material available in the market certainly acquaints them with different skills which are required to carry out the research. Hence, when I embarked on my assignments of imparting research methodology to the students, I decided to give them practice in research skills and practically broached the discussion on how to put different research concepts into practice.

Most books on research methods and methodology provide the distinctions between hypothesis, research question, and research problem formulation, etc. A research scholar undoubtedly understands them. But the problem arises when he is asked to apply them in his study. He gets confused as to research question, its relation with the research problem, research hypothesis and the aim of his research. Consequently, I felt that the best way is to individuate each research scholar's problem and help him frame all these concepts separately. First, the finding of the area was accomplished, then the questions were raised in that area, thereafter, the problem was formed and finally the hypothesis was devised.

Once the session of my training was over in which I had discussed with the research participants different theories of research, the concept of research in humanities, different types of research, research design, documentation, etc. I collected their feedback and then thought to author a book that involves my practices and the responses of the participants of my class. I am research-flagellatingly aware that this work is not going to offer any groundbreaking tips in research methodology, but it is an elementary guide to understand how to apply the basic concepts of research and research methodology to any form of study undertaken as research. The book indeed owes a great deal to all the research writers whose work helped me train my research participants and whose work I have alluded to in this book.

The research in language is mostly concerned with the discoveries of set norms whether in phonetics, morphology, syntax, semantics, or any other area of English language teaching. Language also plays an important part in literary research and enquiry as well as case studies. Hence, various methods of language and literary research have been discussed. The book has been spread over six chapters. Chapter one carries the concept of research and its theories. Chapter two presents different types of research methods. Chapter three deals with research design. Chapter four shows how to conduct research and how to document sources. Chapter five offers suggestions on thesis-making and thesis defence and chapter six presents the glossary of research. The research skills, methods and designs have been explained in simple language and lucid manner. The book will ably serve the needs of those engaged in any kind of academic research.

Syed Mohammed Haseebuddin Quadri

Contents

LIST OF BOXES & FIGURES

1

What is Research?

RESEARCH

The highest form of enlightened activity that ensures intellectual gain at the expense of time and luxuries.

Research is an activity which necessitates distinct definition for different fields in which it is undertaken. It is an activity that enables humans to form an advanced intellectual culture and to manifest human aspirations to reach the unknown realms of knowledge.

Definition

Undoubtedly, 'definition' is an initiatory attempt to understand any subject, though it is worth investigating if it can be taken as an activity of consolidation of understanding of any subject. And 'research', as an activity defies definition, for it is an activity which challenges its delineation in few words. Nevertheless, definition has been still the most prioritized first attempt that most authors employ to make or break their understanding of any given subject in their work. As time, place, context, necessities and sometimes superfluities influence ideas and objects, so also their 'definitions'. Thus, let us define 'research' in relation to the concepts, objects, methods, problems, fields and phenomena which necessitate its realization.

Research is a systematic investigation to discover or invent something; or to evaluate or assess something; or to acquire or enhance knowledge; or to explain or interpret knowledge; or to review or revise the existing knowledge; or to challenge or revoke a view; or to theorize and idealize an observation, opinion, or phenomenon; or to identify problems or questions; or to find solutions and answers to the problems and questions; or to measure the applicability and efficacy of an action or practice; or to make decisions, etc.

The definition of research entails from the field in which it is undertaken. Research involves investigation if its purpose is primarily to find out new things, phenomenon, etc. Research involves creativity if its purpose is primarily to invent something. Research involves understanding if its purpose is to understand a piece of art, nature, aspect, phenomenon, related with humans or non-humans. Research involves criticism if its purpose is to assess and evaluate the worth of any piece of art, literature, theory or attempt in any area of knowledge. Research involves system if its purpose is to systematize any form of knowledge. Research involves problem if its purpose is to problematize any theory, understanding, and methodology; and more than most research involves research if its purpose is to research 'literature on research'.

When an attempt is made to find something, it can be rightly called research. When the thing is found it is called 'discovery'. Discovery by itself is not research; it is an outcome of research. This discovery may be an outcome of systematic attempt or serendipity. However, the purpose of an attempt is unquestionably apparent. That is discovering things, phenomena and facts that others have not yet discovered. The word 'attempt' is central to any research definition. In fact, every attempt to access information, knowledge or wisdom can be universally considered research.

Inventions, in truth are contributions made by the researchers to improve, to facilitate, and to luxuriate human living conditions. Sometimes they jeopardize the very concept of existence, such as the inventions of nuclear weapons, etc. Inventions that are threat to humans in any way whatsoever must be taken as the result of deliberately designed negative research.

If the scientists and technologists are credited for inventing gadgets, electronic or otherwise, then humanities' researchers and social scientists must be credited for inventing experiences, situations, conditions and understanding for humans to live a life of understanding, to foresee the future, and to simulate an experience hitherto not experienced and realized. In this sense research in humanities involves experiential, emotional, and intellectual inventions of functions which can be lived or relived.

Etymology

Etymologically, the word research is derived from the French *recerché*, which was derived from the word *recercher*, which means 'to go about seeking'. "*cerchier*" means to search. Hence, initially it meant to search closely or to investigate thoroughly.

The original meaning is still a significant part of what research stands for today across all the streams of research. None can dispute that every piece of research involves a close search or investigation. The purpose may be any: invention, discovery, understanding, interpretation or revision. Every form of research is carried out due to some derive to advance knowledge. Research is indeed a close search for the understanding of ideas, concepts, phenomena, etc.

Labour, Serendipity

Those who are highly dedicated to research know that research is all about labour. It is central to the very concept of research. It means industry, it means hard work and now it means smart work. If we cannot labour we can never carry out research. Often during the prolong sessions of investigation and exploration, researchers discover something that they are not looking for, but the discovery itself is not any less worth than the thing that they wish to discover. History is replete with such chance inventions and discoveries.

Finding valuable objects, concepts, and results not sought for while research is being carried out, is called serendipity. The chance discoveries form part of most of the studies. However, these serendipitous discoveries and inventions (though some are concealed) come to the fore in the fields of science. However, they remain largely hidden in humanities' research, where the basic idea is to explore experience and increase understanding. We know, by chance we meet some idea, by accident we come across objects and things that enlighten and direct us to develop theories, increase the understanding and enrich our experience of some given field. If we go on record about our chance and serendipitous understanding of any phenomenon or enriching of experience or explanation of complexities, etc. we are pretty honest in our claim to establishing theories and findings. But it takes a lot of courage to do so. Not even scientists own up their chance and serendipitous discoveries and inventions. Nevertheless, as in science so also in arts and literature, the researchers happen to find objects and phenomena that help them explore issues, open up questions, find answers and solutions, prove or disprove theories, understand ideas, explain experiences that they were never looking for. And such discoveries and inventions become the real findings of their research.

Serendipitous discoveries in science are abounding. Alfred Nobel serendipitously discovered Gelignite. Alexander Fleming discovered Penicillin serendipitously. He failed to disinfect cultures of bacteria when leaving for his vacations, only to find them contaminated with *Penicillium* molds, which killed the bacteria. Serendipitous and chance discoveries are also aplenty in exploration. The aim of the discoverers was to reach somewhere else but they ended else where. These explorers must be called serendipitous explorers or discoverers. Christopher Columbus discovered North America serendipitously, while he was looking for a new sea route to India. Thus, the lists of the chance discoveries that are reported are numerous. But it is believed that the discoveries that are not reported are more than the reported ones.

Thus, the question that distinctly arises here is, can the chance discoveries or inventions be taken as research? The answer is in absolute affirmative. Why not? These explorers had set out to find something and in the way found things that were as important as what they had desired to discover. If they had not set out, then nothing would have been discovered or found. It was their labour that took them to places that were marvelous to their people. It was their labour that got them to inventions that helped people live the lives of much improved conditions. Thus, whether things are found by chance or by systematic discovery, toiling is involved.

One may contemplatively wonder about the serendipitous nature of earlier discoveries and inventions, and today's insistence on the systematization of the investigation to discover or invent things in any field of research. The insistence is an outcome of the realization that things will be anyways discovered, but how quickly and how numerously could they be discovered? Thus, researchers in modern times are systematically obsessed with the idea of multiple discoveries and inventions in a short period.

System

Research is all about system. If there is no system there is no research. Today discoveries and inventions are made much quicker than earlier, and knowledge about things is improved much speedily than before. It is due to the systematic approach that researchers have adopted in their investigations. Every industry and institution connected with manufacturing or knowledge-imparting, endeavours to have research and development cell. The reason is the drive to provide quality product to people which undoubtedly in turn shall proffer their coffer. The commitment to quality is indeed reached a point of no return in certain industries. Mediocrity of any kind in any department is absolutely not tolerated. It is this obsession to provide quality product that compelled every industry to have a cell that consistently tries to improve the products of the company in all the aspects in a systematic way. And it is such constant attempts that forced researchers to carry out their research in a systematic way so that time could be saved and multiple improvements can be made in any given product or field.

Motivation

The reason for being engaged in a particular activity is broadly referred to as motivation. This reason can be existence, subsistence, status, power, wealth, ethics, values, religion, service, etc. Any of these reasons may initiate a person into a field of research.

Motivation is the launch of perseverance in the world of attitude. It is a course of strength in human nature. It is a stimulus to action. It is an inspiration to achievement. According to Geen (1994) motivation refers to the initiation, direction, intensity, and persistence of human behaviour.

If initiation, direction, intensity, and persistence are the characteristics that represent motivation, then they become the intrinsic elements of 'research in progress'. No research can be carried out without them. For example, initiation is determined by some desire which initiates the researcher into carrying out research. This desire can be anything from achieving power to serving community. Indeed, it is the research that turns desire into force. Next is direction, which comes from one's supervisor or one's objective. The objective may be anything from receiving degree to making name and money, or to contribute to the field of knowledge. After initiation and direction, comes intensity which is the degree or amount of involvement in the research field. The final element of 'research in progress' is persistence. It is a pledge and an activity of commitment to the research by the researcher. Nothing is expected more than persistence from the researcher while doing research. It is perseverance in action. If the researcher consistently applies himself to the research despite difficulties and setbacks in his way, he becomes the representation of the very spirit of research. Indeed, persistence alone can bear fruits and fetch success to research scholar.

People carry out research because of several motivating factors, such as educational economic, social, and political or sometimes just because of their sheer interest. People, whose aims are educational, economic, and social benefits, are chiefly externally motivated. People who do research because they love a particular area of knowledge are self-motivational. They are intrinsically motivated. They may be highly committed to their likings. The desires and demands in life originate motivation. In humanities' research educational progress or verve to contribute something new to the fields of knowledge often generates motivation.

Context

Research is determined by context. No research in any field exists outside the context. Context in research may be the very demand and requirement to carry out research or it may be the researcher's interest, likes or dislikes. Context apparently refers to place, time, method, position, perspective, idea, opinion, necessity, demand, requirement, setting, situations, condition, etc. in which or in the light of which research is carried out. Context can be understood subject-wise, topic-wise, function-wise, purpose-wise, place-wise, time-wise, etc. For example if I want to get a job in some institution and if that institution demands that I carry out research in the area related to the requirements of the company, then I need to do it. And in such case the true context of my research is necessitated by job requirement or demand. If I am carrying out research in a particular field because I like that field, then the context of my research is my interest. However, this definition of context is external.

Intrinsically, the context of research refers to the study of any problem, issue, exploration of any field, finding out of any solution, etc. from a particular point of view, theory, perspective which may be put forth by some other person or by the researcher himself.

Problems

It is comprehendible if the purpose of research is offered as finding solutions to the problems but it shall sound astounding if it is claimed that the purpose of research is to create questions and problems. Yet, research is just not about solutions, but also about problems. Every piece of research that is carried out in any given field *per se* raises questions and problems. When a research scholar attempts to find a solution to a problem and if he finds it, along with the solution he shall discover several new problems. When he takes up for its practical implementation, there shall show up problem galore. Thus, no research gets completed without it raising and discovering intrinsically and extrinsically few problems and questions. Indeed, that is why, the tradition in research is to create a separate section in dissertation or thesis that deals with the problems that the researcher encountered, or thought or that his research generates. This section is usually entitled 'further line of enquiry', and 'scope for further research', etc. But the main question here is, is it possible to carry out a research just to create problems? The answer is 'yes'. Whether in literature or sciences, problem creation is of paramount importance to further and advance the field of research. The problem creation can be differentiated with problem identification. But hypothetically a research can be carried out just to make a problem or frame a question. This can be called problematization.

LITERARY RESEARCH

Discussing the nature of social research Clough and Nutbrown (2002: 4) observe: 'All social research sets out with the specific *purpose* from a particular *position*, and aims to *persuade* readers of the significance of its claims; these are always broadly *political*.' They also state that 'The purpose of much research at Masters and PhD level is not so much to *prove* things—but more to *investigate* questions and *explore* issues.'

The case of literary research is not very dissimilar. Literary research always has some purpose; it begins from some position and to some extent it is persuasive too. However, its claims are not always broadly political. Its claims can be quite apolitical. Literary research is also about investigating questions and exploring issues. But quite contrary to what Clough and Nutbrown state that research at Masters and PhD Level is not about proving things, the investigation and exploration of questions and issues at Masters and PhD level in literary research, is precisely carried out to prove or disprove, underpin or weaken things, standpoints, views, ideas, phenomena or opinions, etc.

Functions

Research in literature is all about systematization of effort to gain new knowledge, experience, and understanding. If any piece of writing carries any piece of information, the research manifests its application and function for which/whom it is written.

Why anything is ever written? We know that scholars and intellectuals of the world from time immemorial have been presenting information, persuasion, and entertainment as the three purposes and ends of any piece of composition. However, the researcher imparts to us how that composition can be informational, persuasive, or entertaining. In other words literary research is the exposition of the functions of information, persuasion, and entertainment.

Literary research deals with functions of experiences also. These experiences help understand the way the world look at art, and the way the art looks at the world. Thus a literary researcher establishes relationship between art and the world and the world and the art. Sometimes it is an attempt to place art in the world and the world in the art. It is this understanding of relationship between experience and art, and art and experience that the researcher in literature deals with.

Literary Truth

Literary truth is the term I use for the presentation of facts about the text, its authors, its make, its take, its appearance, and its effect. Indisputably the sole concern of literary scholars is to present to the readers the truth before the text, the truth about the text and the truth beyond the text. These states of truth, literary scholars find out through studying all the aspects connected with the text. For example, the author of the text, the context in which the text is set, the purpose behind the creation of the text so on and so forth (here text refers to any piece of writing considered worth investigation). Observing the vocation of literary scholars, Altick (1975: 3) says: 'All literary students are dedicated to the same task, the discovery of truth.' Devisedly, this statement redeems literary scholar and researcher. And I would go a step further and state that all literary students are obsessed with the task of discovering the truth however subjective it may be. This truth is completely about the text and the things, ideas, and people connected with it.

The question is, cannot the readers find out on their own the truth about any literary work? The answer is in affirmative. But it is the literary research scholar, who helps in making manifest to the readers the multitudinous meanings woven around every sentence in a given literary work. These meanings may emerge because of internal or external circumstances that are associated with the work or in which the work is created. Altick (1975: 5) appreciates this aspect quite succinctly. He says:

> Here is a *Hamlet*, here is a lyric by Shelley, here is a *Huckleberry Finn*. Each is intelligible in itself, and any attentive reader can derive immense pleasure from it. But almost every literary work is attended by a host of outside circumstances which, once we expose and explore them, suffuse it with additional meaning.

Thus, the tasks of the literary researcher is to manifest the meanings of the literary text, to make the reader appreciate it, to make the reader see the relationship between the text and the world in which the reader lives, to connect the reader with the imagination of the writer of the text, to uplift the reader to the level of the writer of the text, to associate the reader with the characters in the text, to make the reader identify his attitude in the context and the setting of the text, to make the reader to re-imagine his real living, to make the reader readjust his real attitude in the light of the text and above all to make the reader change his life in this world. How on earth a literary researcher is going to accomplish all these tasks or any of these tasks? The answer lies in his commitment to the presentation of truth through carrying out systematic investigation. Indeed, literary research is all about systematic investigation concerning all the things, circumstances, and phenomena that attended the author and the text.

Literary Investigation

To carry out systematic investigation in literature we must first of all do away with the notions that literary research is quite different from other types of researches; that it is only carried out in libraries, that it cannot be experimental or applied, etc.

Literary research is no different from research in other fields in respect of system. Literary research has to be carried out systematically. Here system refers to either the procedure or the method adopted in the research. Without appropriate procedure no research can be carried out, let alone literary research. Broadly, literary research can be exploratory/basic/pure/seminal/frontier, creative, descriptive, analytical, qualitative, quantitative, applied and action. Or literary research can be the combination of the few enumerated above. Literary research is certainly basic when it seeks to establish a new perspective from a given literary work: whether it is a poem, a play, a novel or a piece of lengthy prose. It is also basic when it develops a theory from a literary work. It is also pure and seminal when it tries to attempt and present a new or novel understanding of a literary work. It is indeed exploratory if it explores elements that are not literally apparent, experiences that are not plainly realized, relationships that are not manifestly related, connotations that are not clearly correlated, and denotations that are not designedly described. Literary research scholars carry out exploratory research by detecting and identifying all the movements, trends, and impressions that surround or affect the literary work under investigation; by identifying and classifying the literary genre of the work under investigation and by studying the elements of the literary genre of the work. The purpose here is to establish the complete or true understanding of some aspect of the literary text. On the other level, literary research is also exploratory if it seeks to solve authorship issues, chronological issues related with manuscripts, etc.

Though some universities around the world are offering research at masters and doctoral level in creative writing and arts, it will take some time before a large number of universities recognize and accept any creative literary piece of writing for instance, collection of poems, a novel, a piece of non-fiction, or a prose composition etc. as PhD thesis or dissertation. This can be considered pure creative literary research. Nevertheless, creative in the sense of introducing a new process of investigation in literature can be found in literary research.

Description and Analysis

Description is an attempt to present the external, apparent features of any given phenomenon dealt in the text. Description leads to analysis. And analysis is unquestioningly one of the primary means to gain the understanding of literary work. Analysis is all about attention. It is an attempt to attend to the work perspicuously and fastidiously to establish its cumulative understanding. Analytical approach to doing research often rejects generalizations.

Research deals with precise observations, not impressions or just generalizations. When a person reads the text very often he makes generalization about the text that he read. He may say, 'It is good, terrific, wonderful, good, informative, bad, boring', etc. A research scholar can never make such statement. Research just does not deal with opinions and judgements, but also with analyzing and explaining the text to convey its meaning and establish an understanding between the text and the reader, and between the author and the reader. A literary researcher does not estimate any work in terms of good and bad. Rather he attempts to present the worth of the work in terms of explanation, understanding and experience. He presents the worth of the work in terms of its inherent qualities that unite it to the world outside it.

Application

Literary research is all about application. We often think a theory or idea conveyed through any genre of literature cannot be of any application. However, is it not that the major part of our life completely surrounded by things connected with literature? Does not the entire entertainment industry around the world exhibit different forms and combinations of literature? Does not the entertainment industry represent action research? Indeed, it does. Whether it is a movie, drama, play, musical presentations, songs, soap opera, or any piece of aired, televised or staged show, it is all about literature and arts. And they are all about applied and action research. If somebody thinks that the entertainment industry deals with creative art and literature, then I must say that it is the literary researcher who actually facilitates the understanding and actualization of all these pieces of arts. These researchers may or may not be persons carrying out research in a particular university for a particular research degree. They may be a small time screen play writers; their job is to apply the art into real life by carrying out research and striking some understanding. Indeed, literary research is applied research. And it is also action research for the literary scholar makes his research benefit the readers and audience for whom it is meant.

Similarity with Social Research

The role of literary research is similar to that of social research. If social research aims to raise consciousness and bring awareness amongst people as to their living, relationship with society, nature, politics, etc., literary research precisely does this. Clive Seale et al. (2004: 5-6) writes:

> The human sciences have an unfortunate history in so far as objectivity, universal truth and science have masked forms of political oppression, achieved in part through systems of knowledge, or discourse that silence certain voices and privilege others. A considerable degree of introspection on the part of social researchers has been prompted by theses views. This has led to a host of confessional narratives in which earlier conceptions of reflexivity (e.g. Goulder 1970) have been taken to extremes, or experimental forms of writing that are designed to make aesthetic rather than scientific appeals to audiences. According to this view, if social research has a role, it is to facilitate polyvocality, assist voices that have hitherto been unheard to find an appropriate volume, generate 'catalytic authenticity' (Guba and Lincoln 1994: 114) and thereby facilitate social change.

And I feel that more than social research it is the literary research that gives voice to the silenced, underprivileged, dispossessed, displaced, and oppressed—politically or otherwise. A literary researcher amplifies this voice. Thus in this sense the role of literary artist is to give voice and the role of literary researcher is to amplify that voice.

The statement that social research's role is to facilitate 'polyvocality' in reality gets represented in literary research. It is the literary researcher who brings to the fore the voices of the unvoiced or voiceless. Polyvocality is truly represented in literary research. Literary research is carried out to make real appeals to audiences in aesthetic forms.

TYPES OF RESEARCH

Research can be classified according to purpose, result, approach/process, and source. Research according to purpose can be exploratory, explanatory, and descriptive; research according to result/outcome can be basic or applied; research according to approach can be qualitative, quantitative; and research according to the source can be primary or secondary.

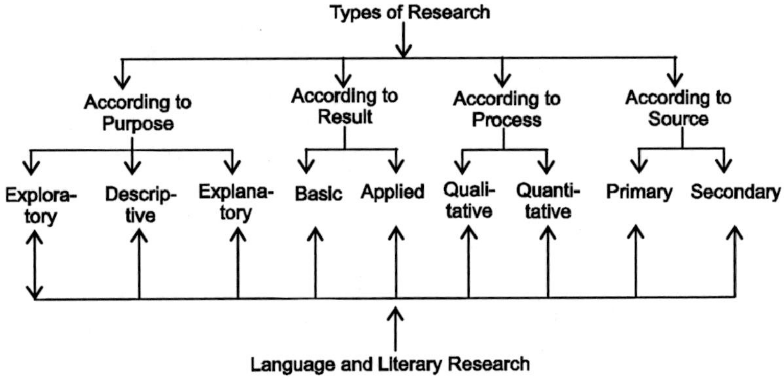

Fig. 1.1

Research According to Purpose

Exploratory Research

Exploration as an activity involves investigation, discovery, finding out of new things, fields of knowledge and ideas. It is connected with searching new patterns of knowledge, ideas, and information. It seeks to gather information about a subject about which no information is available. Apparently all the discoveries that are made either through systematic investigation or through accidents are the result of exploration, for the vital spirit of exploration is curiosity, which impels people to explore and discover. However, the term 'exploratory research', has acquired new meaning in the fields in which it is carried out. The aim of the exploratory research is to access information, to develop hypotheses, to find out ideas or patterns of ideas rather than test their validity and accuracy. Exploratory research is also called formulatory research. The idea behind that is the aim of formulating ideas, insights, and hypotheses from exploration. According to Majumdar (2005: 112-13) 'The major emphasis of this category is to obtain ideas and insights into the problem, to gain familiarity with a phenomenon and the research process or to achieve insight into it.'

Some social scientists define exploratory research from the researcher's point of view. For example, Ahuja (2006: 33) says: 'In this research, the assumption is that the researcher has little or no knowledge about the problem or situation under study, or he is unfamiliar with the structure of the group he is studying.' From this perspective the researchers exploration of anything that he does not know may become exploratory research. However, it can be said that the thing about which exploration is carried out exists, but no information pertaining to it was available and the researcher provided that information. This can be applied to finding out of simple things that one does not know to the very massive discoveries of big continents (though exploratory research in the true literal sense of exploration is not intended in social sciences and medical sciences where it is mostly carried out). Nevertheless, it must be concluded that when a large population is not aware of the thing being explored then only it can be justified as exploratory research.

This research is also carried out in humanities. The purpose behind exploratory research in humanities is to develop an idea, hypothesis, theory or find out patterns of ideas and experiences about which no references were earlier made.

Exploratory research is substantive in linguistics and literature studies. For example, any attempt to find out origins of language, the influence of culture on language, the inter- and intra-language influences, the development of language, the reason of language extinction, the universal aspects of languages, can all be classified as exploratory research. Those researchers who carried out research in these areas knew that research of these topics not only involved the textual exploration or excavation of long hidden and buried texts but also geographical exploration. Additionally, I would call the research in literature which is connected with authorship issues particularly the authorship of the anonymous texts as absolutely exploratory in purpose.

Descriptive Research

Presenting facts, phenomena, objects, and ideas as they are in writing or speech refers to description. Descriptive research describes features, characteristics, appearances of things and phenomena as its nomenclature stands. It is one of the basic types of research. Description as writing technique is employed at every level. No matter what type of research one carries out, no matter what method one uses and no matter what approach one chooses to carry out research, one has to employ description in one's reporting of the research. It is one of the best methods to acquire information pertaining to the problems and issues. Descriptive research answers the question that begins with the words what, who, where, when and how. Though descriptive research leads to the question why, but it does not answer it. Descriptive research is also called statistical research, for it leads to calculations of numbers, frequencies, etc. One of the basic characteristics of descriptive research is, it involves objectives and aims. It does not involve hypothesis. Descriptive research is sometimes intermediary between exploratory and explanatory research. The essence of descriptive research lies in impartial depiction of subjects/ participants or variables under investigation. There should not be any manipulation of these in any circumstances.

In linguistic and literary studies, descriptive research is extensively used. In linguistic research, description is of paramount importance. No matter which aspect of language a research scholar chooses to investigate, he is required to describe the features of that language for the materialization of the true investigation. Indeed all levels or systems of language are required to be described, be they general, like phonetic, phonological, morphological, syntactical, semantic, etc. or specific systems such as, segmental, suprasegmental, generative, lexical, etc. Literary research is not any way free from the descriptive method. Indeed, every literary study involves description. However, when the researcher of language tries to investigate what causes what in any given aspect of the language or literary researcher tries to present the cause and effect relations in his subject, he is no more doing descriptive research.

Explanatory Research

When research is carried out to know why something happens, then it is explanatory research which is at hand. Explanatory research comes after exploratory and descriptive research. It seeks to explain and expound the reasons and causes behind the occurrence of any phenomenon. It involves investigation of the relationship between objects, things, ideas, phenomena, views or variables. The attempt is to provide answer in terms of cause and effect relationships. For example, if speech characteristics with respect to phonetics, stylistics, etc. of second language speakers are studied and presented them as they appear and demonstrating the difference between speech characteristics of native language speaker and second language speaker, then the study is indeed descriptive primarily (though it can be also called comparative research). But when the investigation and explanation made as to why the differences occur between the speech of the second language and the native language speakers, then it is an explanatory research and investigation, as the attempt is to find the reasons behind the speech differences.

Likewise, in plays if the endeavour is to detect the tragic or comic elements or absurdities, and in any piece of fiction if it is to find allegory or irony or elements of modernism, postmodernism, deconstruction, etc. then the endeavour is descriptive. However, when the researcher seeks the answer as to why the playwright wrote tragedy or comedy, why it was staged in a particular period, why the audience was interested in seeing such plays, etc. or why the novelist used postmodernist elements or presented capitalists views in his work etc. then he is dealing with explanatory research. Undeniably, explanatory research is the base for most of the language and literary research.

Explanatory research is extremely helpful for understanding questions related to why and how. It helps in identifying and understanding the reason behind the success or failure of any work of art.

Majumdar (2005: 115-16) calls explanatory research, experimental. He thinks that its aim is to establish causal relationship among variables. An interesting observation that he makes is that causes are not discovered but invented. He writes: "Whereas both exploratory and descriptive studies primarily address to 'what' and 'how' in the research population, the experimental studies seek answer to 'why' such a relationship exists. These studies deal with causal hypothesis or causal relationship. Causes are not discovered but invented." Though in social science one may defend this view that causes are invented, in linguistics research causes are rather discovered, seldom invented or created. Even in literary research they are discovered not invented, even if these causes are not obvious to the author or writer whose work is under investigation.

Research According to Result/Outcome

Basic Research

Basic research is also called pure research, frontier research, fundamental research and academic research. It is mainly exploratory in purpose. It is meant to develop some theory, hypothesis, discover some facts unknown before, etc. However, it does not move beyond theorization part. It is purely academic research. It is carried out in natural sciences, mathematics, social sciences and in humanities. It is undertaken chiefly to establish a pattern of understanding of phenomena, objects, or issues. However, the aim is not to attempt the application of the findings.

Some hold that basic research may identify a problem and issue but it does not provide any solution. But I feel the definition of basic research must include the finding of solution, though application part of it may be distanced from its definition. It is carried out extensively in language and literature, as it aims at the understanding of phenomenon or increasing of knowledge or contribution to the field of knowledge. According to Pauline V. Young (Qtd. in Kothari 2004: 3), 'Gathering knowledge for knowledge's sake is termed 'pure' or 'basic' research.' However, I feel it is basic research that identifies the route to improvement and advancement in any field of knowledge: scientific or otherwise. It is not simply gathering of knowledge for knowledge's sake, it is rather gathering of knowledge for its improvement's or advancement's sake. Basic research paves way to devise and create new applications and actions. Basic research is supposed to be free from any commercial or utilitarian interests. But if pure research is used and applied in real life as a practical contribution of theory then it cannot be free from utilitarian interests. And in my view every research basic or applied is fundamentally necessitated by utility interests.

In science basic research is always placed opposite to applied research. It is pretty much motivated by the scientist's curiosity or interest in a scientific problem or question. In science the purpose of basic research is cited as the expansion of man's knowledge rather than creation or invention of something. For instance, the basic research in science may deal with the question, how did the earth begin? What are stars composed of in the universe?, etc. Though most scientists believe that basic research is required to improve knowledge and to trigger applied and action research, the funding for the basic or fundamental research projects is diminishing day by day from governments and institutions that are dedicated to scientific and technological advancement due to economic reasons.

Nevertheless, the situation is pretty different in humanities, where first of all it is quite difficult to make distinction between basic and applied research. As every piece of research is supposed to increase the understanding, contribute to the fields of knowledge and enrich the experience of human living, existence, attitudes, and aesthetics.

Applied Research

When any research is carried out with the objective of applying it in real life situation it is called applied research. Almost all the fields of knowledge engage research activities for application. It is just not increase in knowledge that has come to be the ultimate goal but what that knowledge can do to increase our standard of living that seems to be the focus of all the research activities in science and technology. Every company pays massive attention to its research and development activities. As it envisions its spread through bringing new concepts and products that help both the company and its clientele. Applied research is tied up with commercial activities and is directed and guided more often than not by commercial interests. Humanities' disciplines like applied linguistics and language teaching particularly second language teaching engage applied research largely. The institutions that involve in such research seek to develop new ways of learning and teaching language or new ways of improving the learning and teaching of language etc. Commercially also, applied research in language learning and teaching has assumed great significance. Particularly because of peoples' great enthusiasm in present times all around the world to learn English. The demand of the English language teachers in China, Middle East and even in Europe is known to all. Thus, applied research is a distinct entity and probably most sought after research in language teaching.

Additionally, with the spread of English and the problems of teaching English to foreigners because of cultural, religious, geographical and attitudinal differences between the aspirants of English learning and the very nature of the English language and its dialects, uncountable number of problems are reported by teachers. These problems throw umpteen opportunities to carry out applied research in language teaching.

Applied research in any field is carried out when a problem or issue is detected. It can best be described as issue or problem-oriented. Its main aim is to solve a problem. Applied research is completely connected with practice. However, one interesting statement of the founding Director of the Centre for Research Architecture, Eyal Weizman really illuminates the true nature of applied research. He says: "Practice is not the result of investigation. It is the tool of investigation." (Qtd. in Jim Rendon, posted Feb. 14, 2007, 'Critique of Pure Research' A new graduate programme at London's Goldsmiths College explores architecture as a tool of social and political practice.)

Research According to Approach or Process

Quantitative Research

The quantitative research refers to the process or approach that is employed in research. Quantitative research involves collection, counting and quantifying of numerical data. It sets out to objectively study and employ any proposition, theory hypothesis or phenomenon. It seeks to study numerically the relationship between properties or variables. It treats the subject under investigation as real entities. It seeks to raise question as to: what, where, and when. Quantitative approach to research involves a systematic and measurable means to investigate the subject under investigation. Measurement or quantification is central to this approach. It establishes a relationship between research subjects and mathematical models. It can help in proving or disproving things, phenomena or objects through statistical details and numerical figures. It commences studying subjects with the help of questionnaires, surveys, standardised interviews to elicit the data for research that can be quantified or measured. Ahuja (2006: 39) says: 'This research employs quantitative measurement and the use of statistical analysis.' In other words the analysis in this research is carried out statistically. Quantitative approach to Research presents findings or results in tables, graphs, etc.

Quantitative research is not only used in natural sciences but also in humanities. In medical science, major research approach is quantitative. Education as a whole must be taken as humanities' field even if it teaches science and technology. Language and literary researches also employ quantitative approach. For example subjects like language enumeration, lexicology, language variations, dialects, language change, phonetics, morphology, syntax, semantics, stylistics, etc. all involve quantitative approach to investigate any given property or phenomenon. According to Burns and Grove (qtd in Desmond F.S. Cormack 1991: 140) quantitative research is 'a formal, objective systematic process in which numerical data are utilised to obtain information about the world'. Quantitative research is objective, deductive, and generalizable. The researcher applying quantitative research approach makes all his observations based on the data that he collected objectively. For example, in language research if somebody wants to measure the speed of the reading of a given subject, then he may record the speech and count how many words a subject or participant under investigation has read in a minute or an hour, etc. On the basis of the data he collects, he may present his observation about the pace of reading, etc. Thus, the observation is completely based on objectivity, etc. It is deductive in a sense that it generates and test theories. And the findings of quantitative approach can be generalized.

Qualitative Research

Qualitative research attempts to understand various aspects of the subject under investigation. The subject may be anything from human behaviour to human acquisition of knowledge. As a research process it tries to find out the reasons behind human actions that affect the world. It deals with the why and how of the human behaviour or action. It is subjective and it does not use quantification but words. It is a research process taken to be the opposite of quantitative research process. In humanities qualitative approach to research is very popular, for most of the literary research deals with human understanding and experience. Thus qualitative research is pervasive in literary studies and scholarship. In literary research whether it is the study of poem or piece of prose or play or work of fiction/non-fiction or even criticism, the objective is to make an attempt to present the true nature of these genres and establish the true understanding so that appropriate appreciation can be made of these works of art.

At times, qualitative research fringes on subjectivity, bias, and slant judgement. Nonetheless, nobody expects it to be absolutely objective. Subjectivity driven by sound judgement is qualitative research's main characteristic. Qualitative research presents realities that people encountered or experiences that people had. Mathematical modelling is avoided in qualitative research. Qualitative research is not undertaken to measure or quantify but to present experiences and attempt the understanding of the subject under investigation. Another characteristic of Qualitative research is that it uses small amount of data to carry out investigation unlike quantitative research that seeks to employ large amount of data to present the results.

Research scholars try to present the apparent dichotomies between qualitative and quantitative research. Hammersley (Qtd. in Julia Brannen 2004: 312-13) makes the following distinction between qualitative and quantitative research: (1) qualitative research uses words while quantitative research uses numbers; (2) qualitative research focuses on meanings while quantitative is concerned with behaviour; (3) qualitative relies on an inductive logic of inquiry while quantitative utilizes the hypothetic-deductive method; and (4) qualitative research lacks quantitative research's power to generalize.

Research According to Source

Primary Research

The sources that are employed in research sometimes are identified with the research. In other words they take the label of research, like primary and secondary sources, which are sometimes referred to as primary and secondary research. Primary sources are un-interpreted, unedited, first hand sources of information. Primary sources are record of events as they are first described or recorded without any commentary. Primary sources are original material on which other studies are based.

When a researcher gets access to any work of art or the artist, he has access to primary source. When a researcher gets the first hand information as data for his research, it can be called primary source. For example if a researcher carrying out research to know the efficacy of teaching poetry to teach a language, and if he goes to a particular class to observe and record the way the teacher imparts poetry teaching, the researcher is collecting primary information, or first hand information. He employed primary source to gather information. This is called primary source. Some of the primary sources are: interviews, direct observations, direct recording of the events, original documents, video tapes, audio tapes, CDs, DVDs, movies, plays, diaries, work of arts, memoirs, photographs, letters, novels, non-fiction, poems, experiments, surveys, court records, etc. Primary research is concerned with the gathering of data that does not exist. It is also called field research by some scholars. Different disciplines of knowledge employ different types of primary sources. Primary source is the original source. It is that piece of art which is neither explained nor interpreted analysed or described or commented upon or manipulated, etc.

Secondary Research

Secondary sources are second hand information. They report, explain, expound, interpret, review, and assign values to the primary sources. They are all concerned with primary sources. If primary sources are the very original documents, then secondary sources are the description, observation, interpretation, evaluation, analysis or summary either in written or electronic form of these documents. Secondary sources offer restatements of the primary sources. Secondary sources include: Textbooks; books, articles, treatises that review or carry criticism on any research work, plays, poetry, biographies, novels, non-fiction or any genre of art; dictionaries; encyclopaedias; bibliographies; commentaries; hand books; data compilations and histories, etc. Secondary sources provide historical background or critical standpoint, in the light of which research can be carried out. However, sometimes distinguishing between primary and secondary source is pretty difficult. The way the material is collected and the purpose for which it is collected also determine the nature of the source, whether it is secondary or primary. For example, an article or write-up in any news paper or journal is a primary source if it presents events, actions, happenings, etc. but it serves as secondary source if it analyses or interprets the events or actions. Research which involves secondary source is also referred to as secondary research. Some scholars call it desk research too.

QUESTIONS

1. Visualize your topic in MPhil/PhD as research activity, and then describe it?
2. Find out the etymology of all the content words that form part of your thesis/dissertation topic.
3. What are the factors that comprise motivation?
4. What are the different factors that create context for the research?
5. What is problem? Where do we find problems? Formulate research problem for the topic allotted to you (or that you chose) to carry out research in MPhil/PhD.
6. What is literary/language research? What are the functions of literary research? How can you identify your research with these functions?
7. What is literary truth? How can you relate your own topic with the literary truth?
8. Bring out the differences between exploratory research and exploration?

2

Research Methods

RESEARCH METHOD

Method is a way or system or procedure of knowing, stating, and doing things. It is also the state or condition of a way, system or procedure. Method is a structured procedure. It is a body of procedure and techniques to investigate any given phenomenon. Method is a means to accomplish an end or attain a goal. The synonyms of method are system, procedure, way, plan, routine, manner, mode, fashion, etc.

Method is derived from the Latin, *methodus,* and the Greek, *methodos; meta* means after, and *hodos* means way. Hence, method is a general and established way or order of doing or proceeding in anything. Method is also used to signify pursuit of knowledge (Almack, 57).

Research method refers to the technique or procedure that is employed in research. Over the years different methods have been evolved to carry out research. Some of these are: the scientific method, the normative method, the experimental method, the historical method, the case study method, the comparative method, etc.

According to Seale et al. (2004: 13): 'Methods are only research techniques. They acquire substantial meaning only in the context of broader decisions involving how we define our research problem, our database, our methods of data analysis and our relationship to those we are studying. These are all methodological matters and choosing a method is only one among them.'

Research Methodology

While research methods refer to the techniques that are employed in research, research methodology is an overall plan of how to carry out research, in addition to providing information about what techniques and methods are suitable for the research under investigation. In other words research methodology facilitates the researcher's understanding of the methods which are suitable for his research.

Some scholars are of the view that research method is primarily about the technique of data collection and methodology is concerned with not only how the data is collected but also how it is analysed, interpreted explained and presented, etc. For example, Ahuja (2006: 41) holds: 'Method is a tool or technique used to collect data. It is procedure for obtaining knowledge based on empirical observations and logical reasoning. Methodology is logic of scientific investigation. Methodology means description, explanation and justification of methods and not the methods themselves.'

About methodology Ahuja (2006: 41) further explains: 'It (methodology) inquires into the potentialities and limitations of some technique or other. It is a plan and procedure for carrying out the research. It refers to research techniques and strategies for obtaining valid information. It is an approach to understanding phenomenon. It is a procedure of empirical investigation. It is not concerned with building knowledge but how knowledge is built, i.e., how facts are collected, classified and analysed.'

According to Kothari (2007: 7-8), Research methods or techniques refer to the methods the researchers use in performing research operations. Research methods can be put into three groups: (1) Methods which are concerned with the collection of data. These methods are used where the data already available are not sufficient to arrive at the required solution. (2) Those, statistical techniques which are used for establishing relationships between the data and the unknowns; and (3) those methods which are used to evaluate the accuracy of the results obtained.

Whereas, research methodology is a way to systematically solve the research problem. It may be understood as a science of studying how research is done sufficiently.

About methodology Clough and Nutbrown (2002: 22) state: 'A methodology shows how research questions are articulated with questions asked in the field. Its effect is a claim about significance....' Here, methodology is primarily linked with the way the research questions are raised with the already posed questions in a given field.

Methods and Methodology in Literary Research

In literary research, methods and methodology are given least importance until recently. In his lecture, John Unsworth (New Methods for Humanities Research, *The 2005 Lyman Award Lecture November 11, 2005, National Humanities Centre Research Triangle Park, NC*) presents this state of affairs in the following words:

> A method is a procedure, or sometimes more specifically (as in French) a "system of classification, [a] disposition of materials according to a plan or design" (OED). In the 1980s, in graduate school (and in job interviews), one sometimes faced the daunting question "what's your methodology?" Usually, what that meant was "what's your theoretical bent: what theoretical flag do you fly?" There was an older sense of methodology still in force, though: dissertations still sometimes had chapters on methodology, and graduate programs in English were wrestling with whether or not to discard requirements for coursework in research methods (which essentially meant bibliography, sometimes with library research methods included). Most departments eventually did do away with this requirement, and by the 1990s, "research" seemed to happen mostly without attention to method.
>
> (http://www3.isrl.uiuc.edu/~unsworth/lyman.htm)

By 1990s again some resurgence in paying attention to methods and methodology in literary research took place. However, one can find handful of PhD dissertations which carry a section on methodology or methods. This state of affair is an outcome of assumptions that professed by critics that literary research is not about discovering new things or inventing new artefacts but it is about intellectual contribution and understanding.

Thus, the situation was such until recently that even the best Universities did not pay enough attention to the methods and methodology part in humanities research. This lack of seriousness pertaining to the research methods and methodology in humanities in general and English studies in particular was discussed by Griffin (2005) at length. She writes:

> In the 1980s when I was a postgraduate student they [research methods] did not figure at all—research was what you did, and the best you could hope for was a brief introduction to the vagaries of the library. There was no sense that you needed to know about the process of conducting research, or that how you did it might influence the outcome, though you might find yourself held to account during your viva for the sources you had used as the basis for your research,...
>
> To this day, and unlike research degrees in the social sciences, for instance, PhDs in English do not require, and in my experience virtually never have, a methodology section—something that is absolutely commonplace, not to say *de rigueur*, in other disciplines.
>
> The situation has begun to shift dramatically since the turn of the century. In November 2002, as briefly indicated above, the English Subject Centre published a research report on *Postgraduate Training in Research Methods: Current Practice and Future Needs in English* (William 2003). The report was timely: it followed hot on the heels of the Arts and Humanities Research Board (AHRB). Postgraduate Review which had appeared in January 2002.... [It] recognised the need 'to nurture research cultures' (AHRB 2002: 3), and 'to encourage best practice in research training' (*ibid.*, 3) (1-2).

By research methods particularly in literary research what researchers tend to infer is the reference is to a set of skills like, library skills, computer skills, reading skills, etc. or techniques for managing material.

Griffin (2005) makes a distinction between research skills and research methods in the following manner:

> Research skills are techniques for handling material. According to the English Subject Centre report which summarised views of staff about the skill set needed for postgraduate work in English, they include search skills in libraries, editorial skills, bibliographic skills, dissertation skills (such as how to structure a book-length piece of writing), IT skills, period-specific skills (such as learning to read secretary script, or how to record variants among different manuscripts), and professional skills such as how to present papers at a conference. (Williams 2003: 58-59)
>
> Such skills may be distinguished from research methods which are concerned with how you carry out your research. The choice of method will depend on the kind of research one wants to conduct. The comparison of manuscripts for authorship attribution purposes, for instance, requires different methods from understanding why listeners to a BBC programme vote for a particular poem or novelist as the best one. For the former one might use ICT methods, while for the latter one might conduct interviews or use quantitative method such as survey. Both are perfectly valid research projects within the field of English studies, a term deliberately used here to highlight the great range of activities which is subsumed under the heading 'English'. ...
>
> Whilst research methods are concerned with how you conduct a given piece of research, methodologies are concerned with the perspective you bring to bear on your work such as feminist or postcolonialist one, for example. (5-6)

This distinction between research method and research methodology put forward by Griffin is very significant particularly in literary studies. Scholars of language studies never feel distanced with the concepts of method and methodology. For most of the research that they carry out carries sections of procedure or methodology in their dissertations and theses, but it is research in literature field that distanced or chucked methodology sections from it. Nevertheless, no research in any field let alone literature can be conducted without involving some method consciously or unconsciously. I would name it a sheer literary nonchalance of literary scholars that to a large extent responsible for it (methodology) being not mentioned in the theses.

If methodology is taken to be a perspective that the research scholar brings to his work, then there is hardly any research ever carried out in literature without it, whether the research scholar mentions it or not. There always will be a section that mentions this perspective, but the issue does not rest with such explanation. Research methodology just does not mean the perspective like postmodernism, post-colonialism, existentialism etc. brought to bear on the work, it means the presentation of over all design of the work, the phases of the research which accepts some perspectives and reject some other, the procedure adopted to justify the use of these perspectives, etc.

One thing that the literary research scholars must bear in mind is that their research methodology may pave way for other scholars to carry out research in similar or different ways which may bring outstandingly scientific and highly verifiable results.

Nevertheless, it must be borne in mind that in literary research let alone other type it is highly impossible to just employ one type of method; the literary research scholar may resort to different and varied methods to carry out his research. This is quite lucidly presented by Griffin (2005), who writes:

> If one decides to write a biography one might conduct archival research, textual and document analyses, interviews and discourse analysis, as well as employing visual methods and possibly even quantitative methods to arrive at the final product. Even quite conventional

> close readings of texts require a range of such methods and skills. Researchers, then never employ just one research skill or method—usually they work with the combination of methods. (6)

Now the use of the combination of methods forms research methodology of a given study.

Research Method and Research Type

In English Studies the distinction is nowadays seldom made between the types of research and the research method. For example, today we talk about experimental method, historical method, archival method, visual method, discourse analysis as research method, etc. However, the question that gets arisen here is if these are methods then what is research? Can we use the term method as synonymous of research? The understood distinction that we make between research method and research methodology may offer a new understanding to make appropriate distinctions between research method, research methodology and the type of research. For example, research methodology is a complete procedure of research; it includes the overall plan, its execution and the results that any research offers. It justifies, explains and interprets why a particular method has been used in a particular research? Or methodology can be understood as a perspective or theory which is brought to bear on a particular study or investigation. In this case automatically research method is the technique or skill which is employed to carry out research, or the technique or skill used to bring the perspective or theory to carry out the investigation. Another important definition of research method is that it is in reality a technique or tool to collect data or information. Now in the light of this when we talk about historical research, autobiographical research, archival research, etc. we are in reality talking about the subject that determines the research and we typify it as historical or archival, etc. Nevertheless if we name it as historical method then we need to give or enumerate or provide the techniques, tools or skills used to collect or gather data or information in the historical research, archival research, etc.

TYPES OF RESEARCH METHODS

Different research methods are used for different disciplines and nature of studies. Research methods are determined by the subject, nature of study, discipline, researcher's subjects (population), resources, expertise, data, constraints (time, money, place), etc. Sometimes, research operations are consistently modified to get the desired results.

Here we shall discuss those methods that can be employed in humanities or literary and language research. Some of these methods are: The Scientific method, Normative method Experimental method, Archival research method, Auto/biographical research method, Historical research method, Interviewing, Case Study, and Creative Writing as research method, etc.

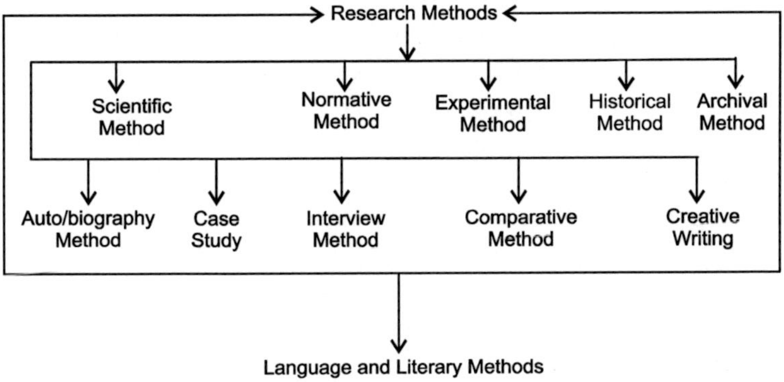

Fig. 2.1

The Scientific Method

Abu Ali Hasan bin Hasan bin Haytham popularly known as Ibnul Haytham (Eng. Alhacen or Alhazen) who was born in 965 CE, and died in 1039 CE, was credited with introducing scientific method in research. He was also regarded as the father of the optics.

According to Almack (2006: 57) scientific method is a mode of applying logical principles to the discovery, confirmation, and elucidation of truth. '*Method* is also used to signify *pursuit of knowledge*, while scientific is used to signify *expert. The expert pursuit of knowledge*, then, comes as nearly defining scientific method as is possible in a few words.'

When the researcher employs scientific method what it means is that he uses objectivity as his tool. He does not use his own opinions to manipulate the result of his research according to the designs of his mind. The discovery of truth, the arriving at the result, all is done with the most detached observations and experiments. The researcher in scientific method in reality suspends his opinions and views, his judgements and inferences until he accessed facts and proofs. There is no room for passion and subjectivity in scientific method. This is the method that is employed not only by the people who are doing research in science but all the people of all the disciplines including arts and humanities.

Scientific method is a general method irrespective of disciplines and the nomenclature that it has got. Here scientific means 'systematic and objective' or what Almack says 'expert'.

Pearson (*The Grammar of Science*, 12, qtd. in Almack 58) says: 'The man who classifies facts of any kind whatever, who sees their mutual relationships, and describes their sequence, is applying the scientific method and is a man of science.'

This statement sums up what does science mean with regard to research? In literary research the use of scientific method is indispensable, if the researcher is trying to get the results or to discover truth based on facts, their relationships, etc.

According to James Harvey Robinson (*The Humanizing of Knowledge,* 57, qtd. in Almack 59): 'Science is by no means confined to stars, chemicals, physical forces, rocks, plants, and animals, as is often assumed. Instead, science includes all the careful and critical knowledge we have about anything.'

The scientific method seeks to arrive at solutions, answers for the problems and questions in ways that can be verified by anybody objectively. The objectifying of the truth that is found in solutions and answers is the ultimate aim of scientific method. No matter what the researcher does, in scientific method his impulse is objective reasonable, not subjective and unreasonable. Subjective, here, just does not mean what one thinks and finds, but what others cannot verify.

Pearson (in Almack, 59) says: 'The scientific man has above all things to strive at self-elimination in his judgements, to provide an argument that is as true for each individual mind as for his own.'

The most important thing that one needs to remember is that scientific method involves investigation. To solve a problem or find an answer, traditionally, people resorted to individual decisions, collection of opinions, the vote of the majority, etc. All these involve anything but investigation. What scientific method did was, to find a solution it employed investigation as the primary tool. The solution is found for the problem through investigation not through opinions and vote of majority. Thus, scientific method gave impetus or set standards to the very concept of research that it involves investigation not opinion.

The Procedure and Characteristics of Scientific Research

When scientific method is employed in any investigation, few steps must always be borne in mind. They are: observation, classification, comparison, and discovery or finding of relationship or otherwise. Experts may suggest more steps to undertake research scientifically. However, the important point to remember here is that the scientific method involves systematic investigation and procedural arrival at the results in logical and reasonable manner which other can get by repeating the investigation the same way.

Horton and Hunt (1984: 4-7; qtd. in Ahuja 22-24) give few characteristics of Scientific Research; they are: (1) verifiable evidence, (2) accuracy, (3) precision, (4) systematization, (5) objectivity, (6) recording, (7) controlling conditions, (8) training investigators.

Henry Johnson (in Black and Champion 1960: 5-6; qtd. in Ahuja 25) has stated four characteristics of scientific research:

1. It is empirical, i.e. it is based on observation and reasoning and not on speculation.

2. It is theoretical, i.e. it summarizes data precisely giving logical relationship between propositions which explain causal relationship.
3. It is cumulative, i.e. generalizations/theories are corrected, and rejected and newly developed theories are built upon one another.
4. It is non-ethical, i.e. scientists do not say whether particular things / events / phenomena / institutions / systems / structures are good or bad. They only explain them.

Robert B. Buns (2000: 5-7, qtd. in Ahuja 25) has presented four characteristics of scientific approach. They are: control, operational definition, replication and hypothesis testing. Control refers to the elimination of simultaneous influence of many variables to isolate the cause of an effect. Operational definition suggests the term must be defined in terms of steps to measure them. Replication means that for the repeated study the data obtained must be reliable. And hypothesis testing means that the researcher systematically creates a hypothesis and subjects it to empirical test.

Steps in Language Research According to Scientific Method

Every method in Scientific Research involves three steps, namely: collection of the data, classification of the data and then analysis of the data. The question is, are these steps feasible in language and ELT research? Indeed, they are, provided the appropriate understanding of the data is established. Supposing, somebody wants to study language improvements amongst the 4th grade students through story-telling. Now the stories that are chosen can they be called data? Yes, but they serve more as means or tools or techniques to collect data rather than the data themselves. The stories denote a method which can be labelled as 'Story-Telling Method'. Once the stories are related to the students and then when they are posed questions, whatever response the students give, their responses serve as data to the researcher which he can classify to find out in which aspect of the language the students made progress.

The Normative Method

Normative research method is concerned with creating new things or improvement of the existing things or state of the things. Normative research method in reality deals with the question what is best for us in any given area of life? Finding out and determining 'this best' is what normative research is all about. Establishing norms is one of the most difficult tasks at present in any discipline. Almack (2006: 115) writes:

The normative science may be distinguished by two chief characteristics:

1. The data and principles apply to values, and
2. There is imminent the probability of applying the facts and principles to affect life situations. The results tend to affect government, education, religion industry and the family.... In the academic field, the normative sciences include law, medicine, economics, engineering, education, art, and political science—in fact the applied and technical subjects.

Regarding the progress in the normative science, Almack (2006: 115-16) observes: 'On the whole, less progress has been made in the establishment of norms than in formulating natural laws. Authority and tradition have been the guides....'

Then the question that arises here is what is to be done to establish norms?

Undoubtedly to set up a norm first of all we are required to know how the things are in their existing or present conditions. Then we can think of improving them. This aspect applies to all the disciplines of sciences. Almack (2006: 117) says: 'The study of the *present practice, of things as they are*, is the first step in arriving at a norm.'

Almack (2006: 117-18) further presents a study which tried to establish norms of general intelligence. He writes:

> Professor Terman of Stanford University discovered norm of general intelligence for American children. He collected ninety items or test problems, ranging in difficulty from tests passed by the average child of three years to tests difficult enough to try the powers of

superior adult. Included among the items were tests of memory, language comprehension, size of vocabulary, orientation in time and space, eye-hand coordination, knowledge of familiar things, judgement, ability to find likenesses and differences between common objects, arithmetical reasoning, resourcefulness and ingenuity in dealing with difficult practical situations, ability to detect absurdities, appreciation, speed and richness of association of ideas, the power to combine the dissected parts of a form board or group of ideas into a unitary whole, the capacity to generalise from particulars and the ability to deduce a rule from connected facts.

The items were next arranged in approximate order of difficulty and submitted to 1700 children and 400 adults as tests. Their responses to each situation were recorded and judged as *right or wrong*, a right answer carrying with it progress up the mental scale. A test passed successfully by seventy-five per cent of the subjects was considered of proper difficulty for the age: that is, if seventy-five per cent of the eight-year-olds passed a given test item, that item was assumed to be of eight year old difficulty. After the preliminary trail, the order of the items were rearranged from the least difficult to the most difficult, as determined by the responses of the 2100 subjects.

The results of giving the tests to a subject were called mental age. A pupil, who passed six-, seven-, eight-, and nine-year-old-tests but not the ten-year-old-tests, was set to have a mental age of nine years. The ratio between mental age and chronological age was calculated, and this was recorded as intelligence quotient or IQ. A subject whose mental age was ten years and whose chronological age was ten years had an intelligence quotient of 100. (Lewis M. Terman, *The Intelligence of School Children,* 2-8, Houghton Mifflin Company)

Now what is obvious from the quotation above is that setting up of norm for discovering anything itself is one of the most taxingly research-filled tasks. It requires a methodology that can challenge the established beliefs and can set scientific norms for understanding or measuring any given field. The setting up of norms for improving understanding or state of things is one of the most difficult procedures. Thus, if any researcher is thinking to carry out research in the areas where he can assess the present condition of a given thing or idea, he needs to look at all the methods available and come up with the norms that can set standards.

Normative Method in Language and Literary Research

The research in language and literature is undoubtedly normative in nature. In language it is carried out mostly in all the fields, for a linguist it is mostly concerned with discoveries that set norms: whether it is phonetics, morphology, syntax, semantics, comparative investigation, or any area of English language teaching. For example, the very setting up of International Phonetic Alphabet (IPA) sound system by International Phonetic Association (IPA) was normative. The choosing of the speakers in any given language to set up phonetic inventory is *per se* normative procedure. Received Pronunciation (RP) which is considered to be the true and the most acceptable variety of pronunciation of English is apparently normative. Without doubt norms are naturally questioned after they are set, RP is subjected to such questioning at present. However, RP still enjoys the title of the most standard variety of British accent and a normative standard to judge and assess the level of anybody's English pronunciation.

Additionally, it is unquestionably an indispensable tool in 'Testing and Evaluation'. The language teaching researchers (particularly ELT researchers) are continuously trying to set standards or norms for testing and evaluation, etc. In literary research norm-setting is a great and critical task. To judge any piece of art or literature, the researcher or critic needs to establish some norm in the light of which the true appreciation of the work can be made. Hence broadly speaking in many cases unbeknownst to the literary researcher, he is carrying out normative research. And it would not be exaggeration if it is claimed that to some extent every piece of literary research is normative.

The Experimental Method

Experiment is an activity or observation made to solve a problem, answer a question, or prove or disprove some phenomenon. Experiments must be taken as a part of scientific method. Almost every research involves some experimentation or other. The Experimental method is also called the method of choice. It is through this method cause-and-effect relationship is established.

The word 'control' is central to experimental method. It involves the manipulation of one variable while maintaining other variables constant. For example, if somebody is experimenting on 'How children behave when they meet failure for the first time in sports?' Now, here several variables are available to him, like gender, age, background of the family, grade/class in which they study, friends they move with, physical strength, etc. Say when the experiment begins all the variables are kept constant, in other words all have the same age, same class, same gender, same friends, same physical strength, but different background of the family. And if the researcher studies the behaviour of the students by studying different family backgrounds of the children, then he is changing just one variable while maintaining other variables constant to get the results. Hence, whatever results he gets, he gets it through changing (not distorting) just one variable. This can be done with other variables too. This is what control in experimental method refers to.

Almack (2006: 145) traces the commencement of experimental method which he likened with experimental science. He writes:

> Experimental science commenced with William Gilbert, born in 1544. He was a successful physician. He insisted upon the necessity of having an experimental basis for all science. His tendency was to put every argument and statement to the test of experiment. When an Italian philosopher taught that iron is magnetized by being

rubbed with diamonds, Gilbert made the experiment "with seventy-five diamonds in the presence of many witnesses", varying conditions many times to take account of possible interfering factors, but he says, "Never was it granted me to see the effect mentioned by Porta."

Galileo Galilei and Gilbert were of the same age. Appointed professor of mathematics at the University of Pisa, he soon found himself unable to sanction the doctrines of Aristotle. One of the views of this philosopher was that the rate of falling bodies is proportional to their weight: that is to say that the body weighing ten pounds would fall from a given height in one tenth the time of a body weighing one pound. No one would lay much claim to originality nowadays in trying out such a hypothesis, but the actual experiment of Galileo was an epoch-making event. From the leaning tower of Pisa he dropped balls of different sizes and weights, finding that all reached the earth at nearly the same time. Reasoning from his results he decided that, except for the resistance of air, all bodies would fall at the same rate, independent of weight. After confirming his first findings with further tests, he formulated the law of falling bodies: *the distance of descent is proportional to the square of the time.*

Experimental Method in Language and Literary Research

It is of great significance if we bring experimental method in our literary investigation. There are several instances where researchers have carried out experiments to prove or disprove theories and claims made by scholars and renowned people. Nevertheless, the question that comes is where is the scope of experiments in literary research? Indeed, there is, if only we look around. An experiment is an activity carried out to find something new, to prove something or disprove something. Suppose, somebody wants to find out what is it that makes a particular author popular and some other author not so popular? In order to find out and determine the causes of the popularity of the author, the researcher may require carrying out experiment even involving control as a means to get the results. The researcher may have variables like, the total work of the author (i.e. how many books he published, how many articles he published, etc.), his style of writing, the taste of his readers, the age of the author, the age-group of the readers of his work, the publisher, the publicity, the presentation, the income of the author from his work, the regularity with which he gets published, his country, etc. When all these things are investigated involving various techniques like interviews, surveys, opinions, etc. and compared with those of the other author, what we have is a complete experimental method of investigation. A mere opinion that this 'author is more popular than that author' does not do here. The experiment may prove it otherwise as well. Thus, literary investigation is an experimental investigation as any investigation in any field of knowledge. This is more near to science in the case of language research. The experimentation indeed in most language and linguistic research is indispensable: whether determining listening, speaking, reading or writing. There is hardly any research in language that just depends on desk. Every researcher of language needs to carry out an experiment in strictly scientific way to get the results. Unquestionably, experimentation in language research has revolutionized the understanding of language and its subjects like acquisition, change, influence, classification, etc. around the world. Today, whether we talk about voice printing, voice to speech text, machine translation, language acquisition device, acoustic phonetics, auditory phonetics or anything, the inventions, discoveries and emergence of all these language sciences owe everything to the experimental methodology.

The Concept of Control in Literary Research

The term 'control' is of great significance in scientific and experimental research. It refers to keeping constant all variables and subjecting a single variable in investigation to get the desired result—desired or otherwise. However, how can one use control as technique in literary research? Where are variables in literary research which can be kept as constant and one variable can be put to manipulation or change? If only literary researchers pay little attention and work towards their research methodology, they will realize that control is one of the powerful tools to carry out their investigation, for it helps in making their investigation specific. Supposing, somebody is working towards the *Marginalization Issues in Indian Literature*. The researcher has several variables here. Let's just take 'marginalization'. Does this refer to people? And if the answer is yes, then it follows in terms of people living in which geographical area, following which religion, belonging to which caste, and using what language etc. If all the variables in the research are kept constant except one, say economic condition, then it means all the people whose issues are dealt in the literature belong to the same geographical area, believe in the same religion and use the same language. Therefore, these variables are constant. Only the economic condition of these people is studied. Hence, the investigation will give result by subjecting economic condition of these people to change. And the topic would be automatically, *Economic Marginalization Issues in Indian Literature*. Thus, by applying the control technique the researcher can get specific results. In other words control in literary research would become a tool for achieving specific results. It, in reality, serves as 'tool for specificity'.

The Historical Method

The use of primary, secondary and tertiary sources to determine the authenticity of the stories, happenings, events, experiences of the past in order to recreate, reinvent, review or repeat them can be broadly referred to as historical research. This activity of recreation of the events of past involves certain techniques and procedures which are termed as historical research method. It is all about learning the past through inquiry; however its aim is to shape the present or future in the light of the past. It is apparent that historical research is mainly concerned with history students and historians. Nevertheless, there is hardly any research that does not take into account history before it starts to make enquiries and investigates in its chosen subject or field. Indeed, when the researcher makes the survey of literature, he is initiating investigation about the past of the subject or subject's progress in the past. Consequently, no research is bereft of historical research. At some point or other history creeps in. Research in any discipline, be it literature, language, social sciences, natural sciences, applied sciences, philosophy, psychology, medical sciences, etc. involves history, without which the understanding of the discipline becomes difficult and in some cases completely impossible. Historical method is often taken to be the narration of the events of the past in the scientific way.

The scientific narration of the past with absolute impartiality is supposed to be the spirit of historical method of investigation. Nonetheless, the truth remains that it is highly impossible to narrate anything in that fashion. We all know history and its narration in verbal construction is very massively subjective. Whether a historian merely reports an event or finds out from several documents and reinvents the events of the past, his prejudices and understanding influence his reporting of the events. For example, if a scholar of the British Empire writes the days of British Raj in India, he would most probably refer to the events of 1857 in India as 'mutiny', when Indians revolted against the British. However, today if that were to report by any patriotic Indian historian, he would call those events as the 'first war of independence'. Thus impartiality in historical reporting is something which is more difficult to achieve than in other sciences. The choice of words, the tone of narration, the prioritization of certain events in presentation, etc. point to prejudices and interest of the historians when they report the events. However, some efforts can be made to investigate and research history without any tilt, bigotry and partiality. If this is done then this itself is a great achievement in historical science.

The Sources of History

The sources of historical research are mostly 'records'. Almack (2006: 174-75) divides records into remains and written documents. Remains are relics of man's activity which has come down from past ages, without conscious intention on the part of anyone to impart information. Examples are arrow heads, pottery, coins, vases, horn cups, battle axes, etc. Written documents are a type of record which has consciously been prepared for the purpose of transmitting information down through the years. The medium may be clay, stone, papyrus, parchment, glass, paper, etc.

It is suggested that scientific history cannot be derived from remains, because it is impossible to produce an orderly series of events from them. Remains are mostly fragmentary, gaps exist in their description which if fulfilled something which is not true is added. For this reason, the days before written records are called pre-historic. The dawn of history dates from writing.

Validity and Reliability of Sources

Historical research is mostly about validity and reliability of sources. Validity of sources is also called historical criticism. And criticism necessitates reading: reading of the documents available as sources. The documents might be available in languages unknown to the researcher. In that case, he requires knowing those languages for mainly it is the languages that unravel the mysteries of histories. The researcher may employ the services of the experts in such languages if he does not know those languages well. The historian also depends upon palaeographer, the specialist in handwriting, etc. The historian depends on all types of experts who can differentiate between the true from false texts and who can establish dates, etc. The history researcher also needs to establish the reliability of the sources: whether the author of a particular text is speaking the truth or not. He must take into account the prejudices, religious fervour, political leanings, experience, education, etc. of the author whose text the researcher is investigating, etc. Mainly the authenticity, validity, reliability are established through the labels of 'external criticism', 'internal criticism' and 'synthesis' under historical criticism.

When a source is under investigation, the historical researcher needs to gather information first of all about the date of the source, the authorship of the source, the place where it was produced, the form of the source, and its credibility, etc.; these are known as internal criticism. Internal criticism in historical method concerns with historical reliability of the source. Here, two things are separately investigated, the credibility of the source, and the credibility of the author. It investigates the eye-witness evidence and oral tradition. Suppose, a text is being investigated employing historical method, from the internal criticism point of view, the literal and metaphorical meanings of the text are analysed. Synthesis, on the other hand, is concerned with historical reasoning. When a source is analysed thoroughly, then the hypothesis is formed which is called historical synthesis.

Historical Method and Literary Research

Literary research depends to a large extent on history. Hardly any research is carried out without history findings its way into it. The widespread use of the term literary history *per se* suggests how literature is connected with history and how it cannot do without history. Indeed, a cursory look into any syllabus at Masters Level in literature in any university around the world confirms that the syllabus is designed keeping history in mind, than literature. The chronological distribution of texts and authors to be studied is practised in almost all universities. And the history of language and literature is given priority in the syllabus. Hence, in literary research, history is an essential constituent. There are several instances where the researcher employs historical method to solve authorship issues, establish authorship, date the texts, find out the origins of texts, etc. It is just not literature even language research also employs history to determine the etymology of words, origins of the languages, etc. Hence, historical method permeates both language and literary research.

Altick (1963; revised 1975) discusses the authorship issues which point to the importance of historical method in literary research. He writes:

> Knowledge of authorship, then, far from diverting the critic from his proper business, lights him on his way. The research that substantiates, or corrects, this knowledge has three chief objects: to identify the author of anonymous or pseudonymous works (or of works attributed to the wrong writer); to decide which parts of a work written by two or more authors belong to whom; and to remove from the received list of a writer's works

> whatever pieces are not his, thereby purifying his canon (the roster of his *authentic* writings).
>
> Positive as we are that Chaucer wrote *The Canterbury Tales,* Thackeray *Vanity Fair,* and Hemingway *A Farewell to Arms,* we tend to forget how many cases undecided paternity crowd the docket of literary history. In some ages the conditions under which literature was written often encouraged, if they did not actually require, concealment of authorship. Before the Renaissance, the poet behind the poem was of little consequence; it was the poem's content and its intended effect that counted, not the negligible human personality which happened to create it. Only during the Tudor period did readers begin to think it important to know who wrote the books they read. But this growing curiosity was frustrated in the case of gentleman authors, who shrinking from what they considered the vulgarity of public print, circulated their work in manuscript. When the anthologies derived from these manuscripts were printed, the authorship of many individual poems, if it had not already been deliberately concealed or lost in the course of circulation was now suppressed, hidden under initials, or simply misreported, and in the later edition the original mystery often was deepened by the unexplained shifting of ascriptions. (73-74)

It is obvious that investigation in literature often involves historical research, but what is interesting to note is, even to determine the authorship issues, a writer or a researcher needs to know the history. The anonymity of the poet deliberate or otherwise and the disinterestedness of the people to know the composer of poem marked Renaissance period; and the curiosity of the public and the response of certain class of writers or poets marked Tudor period. The study of these periods in reality is the study of history. Indisputably literature research is the research mostly of literary history.

Oral History

The passing down of stories, events, incidents and happenings by the word of the mouth; and preserving and recording of them as historical information is called oral history.

Of late, eyewitness accounts, personal opinions, and recorded interviews of the older generation also form part of the oral historical tradition. For example if somebody who witnessed what happened on the very day of India's Independence, 15th August 1947 shared the information with somebody and if that person records it, it becomes oral history for it is based on eyewitness narration.

The authenticity of oral history has been questioned, but at some level one may be wonder-struck to know that almost all histories are basically oral. For instance, if a historian has gathered information about his age, he certainly has not only relied on what he saw but also recorded what other said, etc. This 'saying part of others' becomes an oral tradition *per se*. Thus, one can rightly assume that all historical narration, interpretation, recording, etc. carry oral tradition, that is, information is being passed or collected through the word of the mouth.

Archival Method

What is Archive? The historical records or documents mostly unpublished which are collected as valuable and are considered to be primary source for research and which are preserved for posterity, refer to Archive. Wherever these records are kept, that place is also called archives. One can have from individual to national archives. An archive is different from library in a sense that an archive mostly carries unpublished material whereas library carries published material. Mostly all big libraries have a section of archive housed in them. Such archive is called academic archive.

Archives might contain besides unpublished written material, photographs, paintings, papers, files, financial records, etc. anything that the individual had collected, including published material which was the part of individual's collection, if it is an individual's archives.

According to Steedman (2005: 18; qtd. in Griffin):

> The education system has extended the meaning of 'archive'. A class of eight-year-olds, set to do a local history project, will learn to call the tape-recordings of older people who used to work at the bottle factory, little bits and pieces of memorabilia, postcards and photocopies of ration book, and their own drawings of how they imagine the bottle factory to have been in 1955, an archive. A bundle of your own love letters, a record sleeve and the bus ticket that took you to the first, momentous encounter all make up your own, personal archive.

Here the researcher can see how broad and extended the meaning of archive has come to be used. The researcher himself can have his own archive. Nevertheless, here we are concerned with that archive which contains material of or about the person (or institution) who is the subject of researchers' investigation. The person undoubtedly in at least literary studies would be renowned and a man of literary or intellectual achievements. And his personal things and belongings are considered to be treasure by the government, or institution or those who got influenced of his life and achievements.

In India the most famous archives is in New Delhi known as The National Archives of India. It contains non-current records of the Government of India. It is an Attached Office of the Department of Culture under Ministry of Tourism & Culture. It was set up in March 1891 in Calcutta as the Imperial Record Department. It was transferred to the capital New Delhi in 1911. All archives are opened to research scholars, administrators and even common man if he has any work.

Another national archive is the National Film Archive of India. Its headquarters is in Pune. It has regional offices at Bangalore, Calcutta, and Thiruvananthapuram. It is a media unit of Ministry of Information and Broadcasting, India. Its objectives are to preserve the heritage of Indian cinema, undertake research relating to film and dissemination of film culture.

Archival Research: Archival research is all about managing and handling primary material. Students who require first hand information in their research need to visit archives. The very process of visiting can be really daunting and perplexing. There exist differences in catalogues, system of finding aids, reference systems, etc. from archive to archive. This becomes a little more difficult in India considering the rules and regulations of the archives and the restriction in accessing material for making notes, photocopying, etc. from the archives.

Some of the basic skills that are required to do archival research are: establishing congenial relations with the archivist; learning archives' policies pertaining to sensitive materials and photocopying; and carrying pencils, erasers and a magnifying glass. Hardly there is any archive in the world that allows the use of pen: neither fountain nor ball-point. Most of the archives material no matter how cleanly the archive has been maintained is covered in dust. Thus, bringing a dust mask is a good idea. The researcher must not carry valuables to archives, for bags, purses and any material save paper and pencil are not allowed inside the archive room.

Every archive has its own rules of timing, before arriving to the archive get full information as to when it operates, what are its timings, when it closes for lunch, etc.

Additionally, most of the archives require submission of requests few days earlier for material and its copying: hand-scribed or photocopied. If the archive has any website, browse it in advance. It provides not only information about the rules and regulations of the archive but some archives' websites may enlist the material and documents available there.

Archival research is undoubtedly of great significance in biographical and historical studies. They provide first hand information to the researcher. Indeed, Ismail Kadere (see Steedman, in Griffin 18) says that 'Public Archives were a first building block of modern nation state and national identity'. No matter in what taste this statement is made but the reality is archives are indeed the symbols of a nation's preservation of the achievements of individual, and society. Archives contain material which helps the researcher identify, construct, and present the making of intellectual personality of an individual.

Archival Method in Language and Literary Research

Archival method is essential in literary and historical research. Visiting archives to collect information, by taking notes, transcription and photocopying and then later analysing the information to suit one's objective in doing research are the most common things that the researchers do. These are the few activities that form archival research.

Archive researcher faces some problems while undertaking research. One such problem is highlighted by Steedman (qtd. in Griffin 2005: 27) in the words: 'Aloneness, and the company of the dead we should note, is the very great privilege of the archive researcher.' Since the archive researchers like history researchers are occupied mostly with the things of the past and delve their intellectual capabilities to work out and reconstruct the events of the past, they spend a long period of time in archives which means they live with aloneness.

Usually by archive method what is meant is the practices of the researchers, their methods of collecting information in the archives and learning about the rules and regulation and practices of archives. The literary scholars in archives can carry out the task of finding problems of authorship; examining the evidence, fixing dates and testing the genuineness of any given piece of text, etc. Likewise, archives may be one of the greatest sources for a linguist to study language variety of a particular period and age. Archives can be a great help in tracing the origins of the language, language change, style, orthography, grammar, etc. Undoubtedly, in historical linguistics research, archives can be of immense help.

Autobiographical/Biographical Research Method

Writing about a life which is considered to be worth writing is biography, and if it is written by a person about himself, it is then autobiography. Autobiographical writing involves dependence on memory and recollection or recording of it. It is an activity which is carried out to 'inform' rather than to be informed. Autobiographical writing is an activity of confession which is otherwise verbally protected, and disclosure which is otherwise verbally concealed. Writing diaries is a simple example of autobiographical writing. On the other hand, biographical writing not only employs memory as a tool to gathering information, but also employs documents and records to present the life as lived by a person.

The syllabus in literature at Master levels in most of the Universities around the world is designed mainly keeping the authors in mind, not their works. That was why when any change in syllabus if warranted, the Boards of these Universities that prescribe the syllabus (Syllabus Committees) do not touch the author to study but change his work. For example, in the first year if the students of a particular University have been prescribed Shakespeare's *King Lear,* and it remained in the syllabus for about a particular period of time and the Board of that University feels that the syllabus requires some changes, then this work of Shakespeare is changed with another work, say *Hamlet.* However, the author Shakespeare is not replaced. Therefore, what it suggests is the syllabus in reality prescribes 'author for study' not their work. This study of author mostly comprises MA syllabuses all over the world. This grounding in the 'author study' in reality is the precursor of research that mostly people take up in MPhil and PhD programmes once they finished their Masters. And this is nothing but biographical research.

Undeniably, research in literature always carries the tinge of biographical research, no matter what the aim of the research is and what its results are. The reason is pretty simple, for example, if a research scholar is carrying out research on some aspect of *A Suitable Boy* of Vikram Seth, he would not just talk about *A Suitable Boy* only, but his focus would mainly be on the different techniques that Vikram Seth used in this novel, his collection of material, the things that led him to present such characters in the novel and more than most the life of Vikram Seth, in addition to identifying some character in the novel with Vikram Seth himself. The point is that though the research is carried out on the work of Vikram Seth, the focus of the most part of it would be on Vikram Seth himself, which makes the research to a large and undeniable extent biographical. It is a fact no matter what one works on, a short profile direct or indirect of the author finds its way in the research which makes biographical research very important. However, to establish the authenticity, the researcher needs to be very careful in the presentation of his research. Incontrovertibly, the elements of biography some how find their way in literary research. Therefore, research in biography whether for writing a book or for getting a degree ought to be done fastidiously. A method to carry out research in auto/biography needs to be evolved whether the research is completely (or by title) auto/biographical, or partially auto/biographical.

Mary Evans (in Griffin 2007) in her paper 'Auto/biography as a Research Method' discusses how autobiographies are written nowadays. She writes:

> The modern world, or at least the modern West, has made much of the centrality of education and knowledge to the lives of modern citizens, and so our modern student of auto/biography is acting within a discourse that emphasises the importance of information and claims openness about it as a civic virtue. The individuals who are the subjects of auto/biography live in the same way as the researcher, within a world where the boundaries of the public and the private are increasingly fluid. Moreover those boundaries are often re-written by the subjects of auto/biography themselves, so that what once appeared as a search for information (on the part of the researcher) about a subject is now made meaningless by the self-disclosure of the subject. This raises the question of whether or not auto/biography can actually survive in the twenty-first century, given that aspects of Western culture apparently compel individuals towards increasingly radical self-revelation....
>
> The paradox of contemporary auto/biography and research about it is that in large part the individual life becomes almost less important. That is, the individual

> characteristics of a person becomes precisely that whereas the important question becomes one that is outside the person, namely the puzzle of how a particular individual emerged in particular times. The researcher in auto/biography versed in the necessities of reflexivity and standpoint theory, confronts an individual who is now studied in terms of their own dialogue with their circumstances. (31-32)

Research in auto/biography does not restrict itself to the concept of subject's achievements, efforts, rise to fame, etc. Therefore, the responsibility of the researcher in this method is to find out who are the people who helped the subject achieve things that he achieved? What are the things that oriented him to make some efforts? What are the conditions that determine his rise to fame, etc. Hence the list of outside factors, societal involvement, the circumstances and chance that made that person what he is, are what the research scholar of auto/biography is interested in. In autobiographical writing there are two situations: (1) autobiography as the nomenclature suggests is written by the subject himself, and (2) autobiography as dictated by the subject but taken down or transcribed by some other person. The control of narrations, events, etc. is in the hands of the subject, the one who is taking it down or transcribing it is just a copier or at the most, the one who takes care of language work, that is, style and presentation of the work, etc. But as it is argued by Evans, that in autobiography [of the first type] subjects are moving towards increasing radical self-revelation. What it suggests is that the revelation is just not the confessions but the construction of events that lead to the achievement of some goal by the subject, but the subject is required to present all these in his autobiography.

Auto/biography focuses on individualism though this individualism itself is a part of society and its influence. Evans (in Griffin 2007) who argues this aspect has found unique parallelism between auto/biography and detective story. She writes:

> The most obvious way in which individualism structures auto/biography is in the motive. Part of the psychic restlessness of individualism is to discover the self; it is not an ethic which is content to see the work, the external manifestation of the inner self, but rather it wishes to see and know the internal self. It is in this sense the contemporary auto/biography becomes something akin to detective story. We want to find out why we—and others—act because through this knowledge we might be better achievers in the remorseless achievement culture of the western twenty-first century. (36)

Autobiographical writing mainly claims honesty and truthfulness of disclosure. The researcher, besides studying different aspects of an autobiography under investigation, is also required to authenticate or reverse the claims of the subject (writer). For this, the researcher is required to employ all possible techniques, from gathering information from the contemporaries of the subject to the family members to the organisations with which the subject is associated with, provided the subject is alive or lived in the recent past. And if the subject belongs to the distant past, then the information gathering may begin by visiting archives, work places and by collecting the views that the subject's contemporaries had in the form of published or unpublished material about the subject's claims in his autobiography.

Case Study

When an investigation of the characteristics or traits of an individual, a system, an organisation, an event, etc. is undertaken what we have in hand is a case study. Case study methods are used in almost all fields of research: Medicine, Engineering, Law, Arts, and Language.

According to Almack (2006: 204) 'The case study method is a summary of an infinite number of traits and characteristics of a single individual; a cross section of an individual selected on the basis of some conspicuous quality. The case may be a delinquent, a dependent, a genius, an artist, an event, a plant form.'

Yin (1991: 23, qtd. in Ahuja 2006: 261) has defined case study as 'an empirical inquiry that investigates a contemporary phenomenon within its real-life context, when the boundaries between phenomenon and context are not clearly evident, and in which multiple sources of evidence are used'.

Hartfield (1982; in Ahuja 2006: 262) has given following characteristics of case study:

1. It studies whole units in their totality and not some selected aspects or variables of these units.
2. It employs several methods in data collection to prevent errors and distortions.
3. It often studies a single unit: one unit is one study.
4. It perceives the respondent as a knowledgeable person, not just as a source of data.
5. It studies a typical case.

According to Berger et al. (1989; in Ahuja, 2006: 263), reasons for employing case study method can be:

1. to get intimate detailed information about the structure, process and complexity of the research object,
2. to formulate hypotheses,
3. to conceptualise,
4. to operationalise variables,
5. to expand quantitative findings, and
6. to test the feasibility of the quantitative study.

Types of Case Study

Burns (2000; in Ahuja 2006: 264-65) has distinguished six types of case studies. They are: (1) historical case studies, (2) observational case studies, (3) oral history case studies, (4) situational case studies, (5) clinical case studies, and (6) multi-case studies.

Case Study in Language and Literature

Case study can be carried out in language and literary research. More so in language than in literary research. In literary research one does not notice case study method being employed. However, case study is being employed often unbeknownst to the researcher in literary enquiry. For example, if some body is studying some genre or sub-genre of the literature of the 16th century, then indeed that person is carrying out a case study. No matter how many authors he studies, his focus is on a particular genre. Likewise, if he is studying say the characteristics of the writing of a particular author of a particular period then again he is carrying out case study. Thus, case study method is being employed in literary research, but it does not appear obvious to the general readers.

In language research, nevertheless, case study method is apparently adopted. For example, samples of few speeches or write-ups are collected for analysis in a large part of language research. No matter in which area of language, research is carried out, be it phonetics, linguistics, phonology, grammar, ELT, etc. case study method is dominant. For example if somebody is carrying out segmental study of RP sounds naturally few samples must be employed by the researcher to analyse the data. These samples serve him as subjects, for the variables that the researcher may employ would have to be restricted, if he wants to have control over his research. Likewise, if somebody wants to do research in ELT and his topic may be the methods used in a particular school to teach English, then automatically it becomes a case study for the researcher is restricting his research to a specific school and the methods that are being used there for the effective teaching of English, etc. Hence case study method is immensely present in language research.

Interviewing as Method

Interviewing in reality is a method of data collection. The interviewer gathers first hand information from the subject under study, or from a person who knows the subject under study. The interviewees can be called informants particularly in language research. Though all types of interviews serve the same purpose namely information gathering whether it is job interview or research interview, nevertheless the distinction lies in the preparedness, systematisation and control. In job interview one gathers information to assess whether the interviewee is fit for the position offered or not? As against this, in research interview the aim is mostly not to assess whether somebody is fit but to gather information from that person for the sake of research. Research interviews are research-specific, and mostly controlled interviews. Whether the research is carried out in literature or language, interviews must be conducted in a systematic manner. It is a powerful means of data collection. In literature, if auto/biographical research is conducted, interview serves as powerful tool to collect the facts about the life of the subject. In language research whether purely linguistic or language teaching, interview is the most powerful way of gathering information. Undoubtedly a very large number of works in language research employed interview as technique to gathering data.

What is an interview? The Oxford Dictionary of English (2003) gives four meanings of interview: (1) it is a meeting of people face to face especially for consultation, (2) a conversation between a journalist or radio or television presenter and a person of public interest, used on the basis of broadcast or publication, (3) an oral examination of an applicant for a job; and (4) a session of formal questioning of a person by the police. It was formerly called *enterview*. It was derived from French *entrevue* from *s'entrevoir*, which means 'see each other'. Indeed the former word in English *enterview* is more self-explanatory, 'entering somebody's view' than the present word interview.

Without doubt, entering somebody's view to assess his knowledge, ideas, vision, ability capability, attitude, gumption, patience, perseverance, and power, etc. can be broadly referred to as interview. However, the interview conducted for research is mainly to seek information. Therefore, the fifth meaning (though it can be inferred from the four meanings that OED listed) of interview must be, 'a formal or informal, conscious or unconscious session of questioning of a person[s] to seek information about the topic under investigation'.

Interviews are broadly grouped into two categories: *Interviews for Assessment* and the *Interviews for Information*. Interview for assessment is an interview conducted to assess the skills, strengths, knowledge, aptitude, intelligence, and ability, etc. of the interviewee to choose him for a particular assignment or course. Some of the interviews for assessment are job interview, interview for admission into a college, school, institute, etc.

The second category of interviews that is the *Interviews for Information* is found in the practice of journalism, academic research and police department, etc. Here, the goal of interview is information gathering. The information culled is used in theses, publications, and broadcast, etc.

Interviews are very powerful tools through which useful information is gathered. The employing of interview method in language and literary research is very common and very effective for the results of the research and its analysis and interpretation.

Comparative Method

Comparison as a technique to carry out research is very popular in literary research. Comparison refers to bringing out of similarities or dissimilarities between two works of art, literary pieces, authors, personalities, attitudes, milieus, situations, literatures, languages, etc. Strictly, linguistically speaking, bringing out dissimilarities may be termed as contrastive method, but let us group it under comparative method only for the ease of presentation. However, how can a researcher compare two different subjects? This question is very pertinent. Today we have comparative literature, a field as vast as any discipline. A large amount of work is produced in comparative literature and there are several universities that offer PG courses or programmes in comparative literature.

However, choosing two aspects of any author or work of art is not what usually the researcher is supposed to compare and contrast. They are expected to bring some perspectives to their research under which they must compare or contrast the authors, their work of art, etc. This perspective might be any literary point of view, movement, theory, concept, etc. The researcher needs to bring to his work any of these, and then attempt the contrastive or comparative analysis.

Comparative Method in Language Research

Comparative method in language research is very common place. Two languages, their phonologies, morphologies, lexicons, syntaxes, can be compared and similarities and dissimilarities can be found out. In fact, comparative method of investigation is so prevalent, that to find out the origins of the language, the etymologies of words, etc. it has to be necessarily employed in language research. There are unlimited options available to language researchers in comparative method to doing research. Language researchers can compare any two or more aspects within the dialects of the same language or across different languages. They can contrast two languages which are supposedly descended from the same source or proto language. They can compare two languages which are supposedly descended from two different sources or two different proto languages. The options are undeniably limitless.

Survey Method

A comprehensive view of something formed after a formal study is called survey. Surveying is a commonly used tool in research. The term can be used in almost all types of research. In major research disciplines, the term survey of literature is very common place. It presents the size of the work carried out in a given field. In this sense it is also known as review of literature. And it is the first step towards carrying out meaningful investigation. However, can survey itself be taken as a method of research? The answer is in affirmative. Indeed, if research is assessed in terms of contribution to the field of knowledge, then surveys are true contributions. Survey brings into light new pieces of information that can help in making decisions. Survey itself is a form of research. It is one type of inquiry that helps in formulating a constructive programme. The purpose of survey can be providing information, describing and explaining an event or situation and so on. One can have surveyors in every field: from engineering surveyors to social surveyors to linguistic surveyors. Here, the use of the term linguistic surveyors is of significance. For language surveys are of immense importance to determine the differences in languages, dialects, speech habits, linguistic and geographical boundaries, etc.

CREATIVE RESEARCH METHOD

If research is supposed to make a contribution to the field of knowledge, then no research method can claim to contribute as much as creative research. However, most universities presently do not consider creative research method in literature to be any contribution and thus do not offer creative research approach or method. From contribution point of view, it is quite ironical that the critical work submitted on some author's creative product is considered worth awarding degrees but not the very creative product itself. The need is to offer a course in creative research at PhD and MPhil levels, and accept the creative work in the form of novel, play, fiction, non-fiction, poetry, biography, or any piece of writing as PhD and MPhil dissertations. However, for that there certainly needs some methodology to be developed and accordingly that work may be assessed.

However, there are some Universities like Newcastle University where the School of English Literature, Language and Linguistics (Percy Building, University of Newcastle upon Tyne, NE1 7RU, United Kingdom) offers PhD programme in creative writing and accepts creative work as thesis in the form of a novel, a collection of short stories, a collection of poetry, a play script or screen play written specifically for the degree. The University of Utah (English Languages & Communication Bldg 255 S Central Campus Dr Rm 3500 Salt Lake City, Ut 84112) also offers PhD in creative writing. Some other Universities that offer the PhD courses in creative writing and research are: University of Denver (University of Denver (Denver, Colorado); Ohio University (360 Ellis Hall Athens, Ohio 45701), etc.

Cook, J. (in Griffin 2005) writes:

> The idea of creativity or creative writing as research method may seem a contradiction in terms. Long-held beliefs about the nature of creativity identify it something that is outside or beyond methodical

> thought.... One way of summarising this durable and still active constellation of beliefs is to say that an important dimension of creativity lies in its engagement with unconscious processes. The creative writer has some special relations with these processes, however defined, and this relation is what makes the writer valuable. All this happens beyond or outside established canons of reason and, since the idea of a method is an integral part of the development and the display of reason, method is at best irrelevant and at worst threatening to creativity. (195)

The statement above broaches a very interesting issue that places creativity opposite methodology. Since research at masters' and doctoral level requires a methodology and set skills of certain types such as analytical, literary and critical skills, library skills, bibliographical skills, etc. and whereas creativity is unhinged by any such skills then how it is possible to accept any creative work as research work?

Though Cook has offered good solutions, some take on this issue is, either research skill sets that are required for PhD thesis, etc. must be exempted for creative writing and creative work must be produced as it should be, or research skills sets must be taught to the scholar in a course work, or identify certain research skills that are required for even producing a creative work. For example, if somebody is submitting a novel as thesis and if this novel is non-fiction than obviously all the skills from library to analytical are required for a scholar to produce the work.

Likewise, if somebody wants to write a biography or any piece of non-fiction the same skills are required. The case may be completely different if the novel is an absolute fiction and it is submitted as thesis or if any long poem is submitted as thesis and it is again purely fictional, and has nothing to do with the reality then one may think that research skill sets or research methodology is not required. However, here also it is advised that the research scholars can develop the glossary, use of allusions, meaning of certain characters and their significance, etc. Thus, no matter what type of creative writing is being carried out, research skill sets are always required. Hence the suggestion that the creative piece of writing as PhD or MPhil thesis can have all the ingredients of any research thesis is tenable. And it makes it more comprehensive and systematic. Even if the work of art or creative writing is completely fictional, the trend nowadays in literature is to bring out the work in such a way that it becomes linguistically easy for the readers to understand, for appreciation always rests on understanding. The works of writers like, Tolkien, Vikram Seth, and the famous Rowling undoubtedly require some elucidation. Here, the explanation part in the form of historical or mythical allusions, glossary and bibliography are required, which make the work creative but research-based. Thus, if any scholar is submitting a novel as thesis, then he ought to present the novel in such a way that makes its reading easy, understandable and enjoyable, and for that he has to unquestionably follow some conventions of research, like providing explanation of allusions, providing glossary, etc.

ECLECTIC RESEARCH METHOD

We know that the labelling of research after a particular method is done bearing in mind the dominant features of that method used in the research. Nevertheless, the researcher uses other methods or techniques of other methods in his research. However, he may or may not specify or give credit or representation to the techniques of other methods that he used while carrying out his research. For example, somebody might take up the issues of cosmopolitanism in literature and according to the process of research he may label it as qualitative research. For, in addition to the information available in the books that he used as his sources to discover the issues related with cosmopolitanism, he may take interviews and gather data in words to strengthen his arguments, conclusions, etc. However, along with that if he gives the statistics about issues that the cosmopolitans face from the work and the people whom he interviewed, then his research would enter the realm of quantitative research. Likewise this research may simultaneously employ the techniques of interview methods, etc. In the discussion to the methodology he may not mention all these methods that he knowingly or unknowingly employed. Still he used more than one method to carry out his study and investigation. But when we consciously use these methods and discuss them in the research methodology chapter and give justification, it shows an eclectic use of techniques available to us to carry out our investigation. And I feel that the use of more than two methods in any research must be termed as eclectic method. The purpose is to arrive at the truth in the best possible manner employing all or several or necessary methods in any given field of research. Thus, eclectic method is the conscious use of different methods to carry out research.

QUESTIONS

1. Bring out the difference between method and methodology in the light of your research.
2. Discuss the importance of method in literary research?
3. Discuss different types of research?
4. Which type of method is suitable for your research and why?
5. 'Literary research is a desk research; it is completely theoretical and has nothing to do with any sort of application or action.' Invalidate this statement with reasonable arguments and examples.
6. Enumerate the differences between archival research and historical research?
7. Why comparison has become the most popular and easy way of carrying out research in literature? What substantive contribution can comparison make? Discuss.
8. Discuss 'creative writing as research discipline'.

3

Research Design

RESEARCH DESIGN

Research design refers to the complete plan in accordance of which the research is carried out. It is a procedural layout of research. It involves arrangement of different phases or stages of research. It stretches from the idea of research conception to the very practice of research execution. Research design deals with question such as: How to select research topic or area? What is the aim of the research? What methodology or procedure must be adopted to carry out the research? How the research question is formulated? How the hypothesis is devised? What is research proposal? What methods are employed to collect the data for the research? How the analysis is carried out? How different resources are utilized? And so on.

Research design is a planned anticipation of the situations that arise in any given research study, and an answer to how these situations can be tackled. It is a scheme of conducting research.

Every research that aims at some contribution in the field of knowledge certainly comes out with a distinct research design, absolutely tailored to the requirements of that research, its result, and its purpose. In other words, with the new findings of the research, new research designs emerge.

Claire Selltiz et al. (1962: 50) writes: 'A research design is the arrangement of conditions for collection and analysis of data in a manner that aims to combine relevance to the research purpose with economy in procedure.'

Research design is an educated outline of the research. It deals with everything that is connected with the research. It allows for the possible set backs in research as well. It is a guesswork map put on record so that research can be carried out systematically with minimum of diversions. Research design deals basically with research problem, the study of the subjects/participants, procedure adopted to gather data, and the analysis of the data.

Research Design in Literature

In literary research, the designing of research is as important as in science and technology. However, it is observed that literary scholars pay least attention to research designing. They, no doubt, possess the idea what they want to do, but are most reluctant to do so. Since most of the research is taken (undoubtedly wrongfully) to be desk research in literary studies, the literary researcher does not show any interest in designing any research lay out of his work. I am making these observations on the basis of my personal experiences as supervisor. Literary scholars hardly motivate themselves to have any plan of their research. One of the argument-cum-question that I frequently receive is how can we plan something that we have not yet read? My answer to these literary researchers is simple, 'if you are referring to the topic on which you want to do research, then I am compelled to say that research is not your cup of tea. Because even for tentative formation of the topic you are required to do enough reading (particularly in literary research) without which you cannot think of carrying out any investigation. And if you are talking about the very nature of research that you cannot really plan anything in literary research for new things emerge and new ideas are found that help in the formation of research procedure; and only in the end can you come out with the appropriate plan of research. I feel this line of thinking is centrally flawed. It is not so that you can get the real plan in the end. You need to have a plan; this plan as the new things emerge or are encountered gets modified; and this modification every researcher knows is the mark of research progress.' Another thing is that in literary research the chances are pretty less than in the research fields of science where because of different results the researchers are required to constantly modify some elements of their research plan. Thus, research design in literary research helps in developing a step by step approach to the operationalisation of research.

Research design is a plan before hand for a step-by-step process of carrying out research. When the research is in progress it is pretty common to backup, revise, add material or modify the research topic. This is necessarily hinged on the discoveries that the researcher makes during research. Research design is unquestionably a skeleton which is fleshed out during the research. It is a plan for the identification of the problem, the location of the means to solutions, the assessment of the data used to reach the solutions, the analysis of the data, the development of the solution and finally the expression of the solution.

In literary research, all these steps are employed. First identification of the problem is made. Suppose, if somebody wants to work on Mark Twain's *Adventures of Huckleberry Finn* and after thorough reading of it finds 'patronizing' as an issue worth investigating in relation with the 'antebellum society'. Thus, the researcher has identified a problem. But the researcher is required to turn this problem into a genuine problem statement or question. Next he is supposed to locate the means to solutions. In this case the solution might be to prove that Mark Twain was trying to patronize dark-skinned people and for that he chose the character of Huckleberry Finn and Tom Sawyer to condescend Jim who was a run-away slave, in the garb of helping him. What are the means that the researcher is required to collect to prove his point? The use of primary source, which is the novel itself, the use of secondary sources such as criticism on him, the study of antebellum society, probably meeting people who have devoted their lives to the study of Mark Twain, visit to the locations, etc. Subsequently, assessing and analyzing the data collected, then the development of the solution which may prove that Mark Twain was trying to patronize the blacks and finally the documentation of it.

Literary research is basically committed to developing the understanding and enriching the experience of the text, its various aspects, its author, and its audience. Thus, in literary research, the problem is mostly formulated in such a way that the solution of which is supposed to develop and increase the understanding of the text, its world and the world outside it. If literary research is all about relationship between experience and understanding, then the research design in literary research is expectancy arrangement and execution of that relationship.

RESEARCH PROBLEM

Problem is a tension between the present state and the desired state. It is an unresolved issue or situation. The general meaning of problem can be understood from synonyms like hindrance, obstacle, difficulty, interruption, obstruction, impediment, barrier and hitch in a way to achieve a desired purpose or reach a destination, etc. However, research problem is just not any obstacle or impediment in a way to achieve one's goal, but it is a condition that leads to resolving a difficulty, situation, condition and obstacle. In other words, research problem is a 'problem' about a problem.

Almack (2006: 31) writes: "The term [problem] comes from the Greek, *proballein*: anything thrown forward... a question proposed for solution; a matter stated for examination or proof; a matter difficult of solution or settlement; a doubtful case or question. Problem is frequently used as synonymous with project. The derivation of the latter is identical, except that it is from the Latin and seems to have been modified to mean: 'to throw forward in a prescribed direction'."

Research, no matter of what type, is supposed to take us forward. And it is the etymological meaning of problem which best captures the real spirit and purpose of research. R.S. Woodworth (qtd. in Almack 2006: 31) brings out the psychological aspect of the problem in the following words: 'a situation for which we have no ready and successful response by instinct or by previously acquired habit. We must find out what to do.'

Johan Dewey (qtd. in Almack 2006: 32) says that every conscious situation involves the possibility of change. 'The need of clearing up confusion, of straightening out an ambiguity, of overcoming obstacles, of covering the gap between things as they are and as they may be when transformed, is, in germ, a problem.'

'Problem' is a situation for which we do not have any answer yet. We need to find an answer for it. Accordingly, a research problem is a situation, which presents complex, puzzled and discomfited state of knowledge. It is a context which seeks solutions. It is a condition which prompts questions and hunts for answers and solutions. Every type of research is necessitated by problem situation. This problem situation can be broadly called problem area. The problems in research can be identified severally. However, the central means are reading, observation, and experience. When a researcher reads literature (in whatever the area he wishes to do the research) he may find certain things missing, or inadequately represented, or carry flawed arguments, etc. now, he has the research problem. Secondly, when he observes some area visually, or by any means, connected with any sphere of life and finds that certain things are not covered, he has a research problem. And thirdly, when he experiences things or phenomena or observes others experiencing them and finds that there are shortcoming and misgivings in the situation connected with the experience, and something can be done to improve the nature of experience or things and ultimately his own experience of them, then he has a problem. There are numerous situations that supply problems to researcher, if only he observes.

Problem Formulation

In research one just does not encounter a problem by chance, but sometimes (and more so in literary research) one creates problem to solve problems. In other words, anything can be *problematized* in research to solve the problems. And research type like, exploratory or basic, rather tries to develop a problem.

The turning of any situation or condition into a problem or developing a problem to improve any situation can be referred to as problem formulation.

Problem formulation is of utmost importance in any research. To find the correct solution the researcher needs to have the right problem. Problem formulation helps in the collection of appropriate data, contacting right respondents/subjects/participants, working within the stipulated time and schedule, and defining the boundaries of research. The problems can be defined or formulated by researcher himself through posing questions in his area of interest. However, if the research problem is given by any organisation or institution it is completely a different matter. In such case the researcher gets more involved with studying and understanding the research problem.

Zikmund (1988: 67) says that the selection of the problem of research must be linked with the following: What is the purpose of the study? How much is already known? Is additional information necessary? What is to be ascertained/ measured? How is it to be measured? Can the required data be collected, i.e. will the respondents give the correct information? Is the present time appropriate for undertaking research? Can a hypothesis (tentative proposition) be formulated? Is time/money adequate for the research?

In the light of the questions that Zikmund states for the selection of research problem it can be said that the aim of the study shall determine the researcher's efforts to choose the problem. Next he must know the extent of information available in the area he wishes to study so that he can concentrate on things that are not known yet. Then he must also think about what is it that he requires to study, measure, assess or analyse, etc. After that he must think about the techniques to be employed for measuring and analysing the data. And finally he needs to also take into account the time, and respondents'/subjects' constraints, etc.

Sources for Finding Problems

Who will supply problems? Where to find them? What should be done to find problems?, etc. are some of the questions that perplex every researcher? But all he requires to find the problem is observation and acumen. The subjects and topics are infinite and unending as the interests, fantasies, imaginations, desires, and activities of human beings. The prerequisite to discovering a problem is the verve and enthusiasm to make some contribution in the world, to solve some issue, to facilitate living condition, to improve quality of understanding and to share experiences.

Finding an original problem itself is a research discovery. A potential research scholar can find problems in nature, human actions, his observations, his experiences, the experiences of others, his necessities, others' necessities, his superfluities, others' superfluities, etc.

One best way to find problems is to have lots of questions. Pose these questions to teachers, experts, specialists in the area, etc. and if the researcher feels that the answers that he received are not adequate and do not satiate then he has research problem at hand.

Faraday (qtd. in Almack 2006: 43) says: 'I had a very lively imagination and could believe in the Arabian Nights as easily as the Encyclopaedia. But facts were important to me and served me. I could trust a fact, and always cross-questioned an assertion.'

What it suggests is, to a scientist's facts are always important not the legends that the imagination weaves. However, for a researcher it is just not facts that are important but a lively imagination also. For, this imagination makes the researcher dream; and to achieve that dream he may carry out a research which paves way even to the established scientists to search for the unthinkable and undiscoverable.

However, for the literary researcher more often than not, the imagination that concocts myths itself serves as the problem for research. For through these myths, the literary researcher tries to unravel the mysteries of the mind that makes it. The researcher as an observer and a discerner presents his efforts as solution to the problems that these myths generate.

Thus, for the literary researchers the sources for finding research problems are very many.

Almack (2006: 48) suggests four headings to find problems. They are: (1) Analyze what is known, including the historical record; (2) Look for gaps or deficiencies in explanations—that is, for "areas of darkness"; (3) Watch for incongruities and contradictions, the points of controversy, the untested conclusions; and (4) Follow clues and suggestions obtained from reading, conferences, and thinking. Observe where activity is greatest, and where there is evidence of neglect. Keep a memorandum of ideas, hypotheses, and problems as they occur.

Given below are few situations where the research aspirant may get the problems to initiate his research.

Seminars/Workshops/Symposium

A prospective researcher must attend as many workshops, seminars, conferences and symposiums as he can. For during presentations, discussions, paper reading sessions, scholars throw light on different topics, subjects, areas of potential research, sometimes deliberately and sometimes unwittingly. This helps him to think about the areas and to read some literature, which in turn helps him to formulate a research problem. Recently I attended a workshop on Academic Publishing. There was a panel discussion, where one of the participants disclosed that in literature a research has been carried out on medical romance: that is the researcher has collected few novels which deal with the romance of doctors or medical persons. Indeed, I found the topic so interesting that I started thinking about getting research done on the same lines in technology romance, law romance, crime romance, etc.

Discussion with Teachers and Specialists

Another potential source for getting research problem is discussion and meeting with people connected with the researcher's subject. Sometimes teachers can provide a large number of research topics and problems. The source for teachers' gathering of problems is their reading, and teaching experience. They literally encounter umpteen number of problems which if they are really research oriented share with the student to turn them into real research problems. Therefore, teachers, experts, specialists of a given field can be the liveliest sources to get the research problems.

Theses/Dissertations

Going through theses and dissertations also help immensely to find research problems. Mostly the section 'further line of inquiry' or 'scope for further research' illuminates different areas where research can be carried out. Thus, every potential research scholar must go through as many dissertations as he can to get the idea about research problem.

Books/Journals/Periodicals

Truly research problem emerges and takes shape from perusing books, articles in journals and periodicals. Inadequacy is the condition which emanates problems in any given area. If the researcher finds that the information is wanting in a particular area, he can straightaway have a problem at hand. But reading books and journals profusely are a must for a potential researcher. This reading leads him into problem area and topic selection and it serves as an initial review of literature for him. Mostly people think that review of literature is done only after deciding the topic. But every prospective researcher must know that the literature search begins before he finds his problem and decides his topic.

Problem Formulation in Language and Literary Research

Does literary or language research require problem formulation? The answer is yes it does. No matter what area a particular researcher has chosen to undertake the research, he must either identify the problem or formulate the problem. It is the problem that every researcher in every field studies either to solve it or to explain it. Since literary research is primarily undertaken to understand a literary work or find out new meanings of the work or explain a new experience or theory to the readers of the work, etc. the problems are there aplenty.

Understanding, experiences and establishment of relationships throw numerous problems. And if the researcher wants to develop new understanding of the literary work, then he is required to problematize the current understanding of the work? Hence, the problem is there if a researcher wants to attempt a new understanding of it.

It is also very important that the researcher must consult his supervisor or some expert in the area in which he is planning to undertake his research before he formulates the problem. The consultation with the supervisor improves the understanding of the nature of the problem and helps in devising it facilely. In language research, mostly problems are available abundantly. Formulation in terms of turning something into an issue or problem is rare. However, this is also happening frequently in language research. For example, say somebody has carried out a research on the 'Suprasegmental Features in the Speech of Hindi Speakers of English'. On the same lines a researcher may, whose mother tongue is Assamese, wish to work on 'The Suprasegmental Features of Assamese Speakers of English'. Though there may be plenty of problems available but here the researcher needs to observe first, few characteristics of Assamese Speakers' English and then formulate a problem. Nonetheless, problems in language research are very numerous. Educational institutions, research organisations, often advertise the problem areas in which research can be carried out.

RESEARCH QUESTIONS

In every type of research, the problem is stated mostly through questions. Identifying research problem means posing research questions to be answered. In other words there may be several problems in research but formulating appropriate research questions is important for specifying the correct research problem and finally seeking appropriate answers. Research questions delineate the scope and limitation of research.

Blaikie (2000: 23; qtd. in Ahuja 2006: 115) says that the formulation of research questions is the real starting point in preparation of a research. The questions have to be related to three aspects: what, why, how? 'What' questions seek description, 'why' questions seek explanations and understanding, and 'how' questions seek interventions to bring about change.

Hedrick et al. (1993: 22-23; qtd. in Ahuja 2006: 116) have identified four types of research questions: descriptive, normative, correlative and impact.

A researcher may begin his research with a general question but he keeps refining it until he gets appropriate question. Or he may have several questions that he wishes to answer through his research. Research questions are substantive means of presenting the research problem. One may wonder, 'what is the difference between research problem and research question'? The difference is research question helps formulate research problem. The research problem can be expressed through research question. Or one research problem may have several research questions. And in certain cases research problem itself is research question. In other words in research if there is a problem the researcher seeks to solve it; if there is a question he attempts to answer it and if there is a hypothesis he tries to prove it or disprove it.

HYPOTHESIS

Literally and etymologically, hypothesis means a placing under. It is derived from the Greek *hupothesis* where *hypo* means 'under' and thesis means 'a placing', 'a proposition'.

Any supposition, assumption, proposition, idea, predictive statement, well thought-speculation, explanation, educated conjecture or guess which has not been tested yet to prove or disprove its validity can be called hypothesis. In research, hypothesis is presented in the form of explanation or tentative answer, or proposal.

Hypothesis is a tentative statement asserting a relationship between certain facts, whose validity is unknown.

According to Kothari (2007: 184), 'Hypothesis is usually considered as the principle instrument in research. Its main function is to suggest new experiments and observations. In fact, many experiments are carried out with the deliberate object of testing hypotheses.'

In qualitative research, hypothesis emerges out of the research, in quantitative research, hypothesis is tested to be proved or disproved.

J.S. Mill (qtd. in Majumdar 2005: 79) explains:

> A hypothesis is any supposition which we make (either with actual evidence, or an evidence avowedly insufficient) in order to endeavour to deduce from it conclusions in accordance with the facts which are known to be real, under the idea that if the conclusions to which the hypothesis leads to are known truths, the hypothesis itself either must be true or at least is likely to be, true.

However, there are certain cases where hypothesis is particularly put to test to prove it wrong, or to disprove it.

Types of Hypotheses

Hypotheses are classified into several types like, working hypothesis, research hypothesis, evaluating hypothesis, scientific hypothesis.

Working hypothesis is the initial tentative assumption or supposition of the researcher. As he works, he collects information, he reviews related literature and he refines it into a final research hypothesis.

Research hypothesis is a researcher's supposition, assumption or proposition about some phenomenon. He wants it be disproved.

Evaluating hypothesis involves those propositions which are framed in such a manner that scientists can prove them wrong. They are also called falsifiable. They involve hypothetico–deductive method.

Scientific Hypothesis is based on an empirical data. They are taken as tentative or trail solution to a problem or a tentative explanation of some phenomenon.

DIFFERENCE BETWEEN RESEARCH PROBLEM, RESEARCH QUESTION, RESEARCH AIM AND HYPOTHESIS

Sometimes in Research we have a research question as well as research hypothesis. It depends upon the research scholar to make the distinction between these two. Research question is not research hypothesis. It is obvious from the objectives of both. A question always seeks an answer and a hypothesis is always tested.

The Research Problem, Research Questions, Research Aims/Objectives and Research Hypothesis are all interrelated. Let us strike some distinction among them for complete understanding of research framework.

Research Objective refers to the purpose or aim behind undertaking research. *Research Problem* involves a situation or phenomenon where the problem or issue lies. *Research Question* involves questions such as what, how, where, when, etc. to find out the nature and extent of the problem or issue. And *Research Hypothesis* seeks to provide tentative explanation or tentative answer to the research question, which during the course of research stands proved or disproved.

Let us have an example so that a clear outline of the distinctions among them can be understood in a nutshell. I have taken the outline of the table from Ahuja (2006: 118), and proposed an example of the problem, question, objective and hypothesis in the Box 3.1.

Anybody can notice the functional distinctions lay between any of the headings in the box above.

My advice to every potential researcher is to first frame this table when they set out for the research, it helps them progress steadily in their research. And this table itself can be taken as tentative or working, till the final, refined and appropriate questions and hypotheses can be formulated. This box can be of great help even at the level of defending one's research proposal or at the end for the research defence/*viva voce* examination.

Box 3.1: Distinction between Research Problem, Research Question, Research Objective and Research Hypothesis

Research Problem/Area	Research Questions	Research Objectives	Hypothesis
Teaching Poetry to Engineering Students	Do engineers learn anything from poetry? How poetry can be taught to engineers? What aspects of the poems must be highlighted? Whose poems best suit to the engineering students? What teaching techniques must be adopted? So on and so forth.	To Make engineering students be in touch with Arts so that they can bring aesthetic value to their profession	Engineers learn style through poetry. By reading poetry engineers learn how to appreciate beauty and carry this to their profession. Engineers will connect their profession to the arts and humanities etc.

RESEARCH PROPOSAL

Research proposal is a written plan to carry our research. Submission of a research proposal for MPhil and PhD programmes is necessarily conditioned in most universities, irrespective of whether the research is financially sponsored, self-financed or pursued for any other reason. Research proposal is also called synopsis in some universities. Before admitting any student into any doctoral or lead in-to-doctoral course like MPhil universities ask the prospective research candidate to submit his research proposal. Mostly research committee or admission committee or the department in which the candidate seeks admission, goes through the research proposal and considering its soundness, relevance and contributing nature to the discipline or very field of knowledge the admission is granted or denied. The research proposal is also required to be defended in oral or *viva voce* test. This is the normal procedure; however, different universities around the world use different methods to select candidates for their research programmes.

One of the important things that the potential researcher must bear in mind is that his proposal must give the sense that it shall be a contribution to knowledge.

An outline of research proposal can be as follows:

- A Title
- A Research problem/ Research question
- Hypothesis
- Limitations and delimitations of the study
- Definition of terminology
- Significance of the study
- Review/survey of related literature
- Time schedule
- Budget requirement (where applicable)
- Bibliography or resource list

Title

Though research title or topic comes first in any proposal but it is devised after understanding the research problem, question and hypothesis. It is always prudent to devise it after clearly stating all these. The title must refer to what is researched, how it is researched, where it is researched when it is researched and why it is researched. It must also state the possible solution though tentative.

For example, the topic "Love and Excess? Women's Scandalous Fiction, and the Feminine Ideal of Moderation, 1680-1730" carries most of the essentials in it:

Terra Caputo, (the University of Miami) is working on this topic. Though the research is in progress but from the title one can find a large chunk of what is required as research can be seen: first, the answer to 'what is researched?' is found in the part of the title "Love and Excess? Women's Scandalous Fiction...." Next the answer to 'how it is researched?' can be easily seen through the title's feminist perspective, this aspect mostly throws light on the methodology. Why it is researched can be answered by the scholar for it in reality lays emphasis on the aims of the research, but from the title it can be inferred that to demonstrate the "Feminine Ideal of Moderation". And thereafter when it is researched can refer to either the time when the research is carried out or the time to which the research is limited; here the title refers to the latter

'1680-1730'. And finally where refers to the place where the research is carried out or the context in which the research is undertaken. In this case, the context could be women's 'Scandalous Fiction'.

Research Problem/Research Question in Research Proposal

In the proposal the research problem or research question is fundamentally tentative. When the admission is granted, the research problem is mostly reworked. As the researcher thinks and reads literature, his understanding increases and he sees the problem from improved perspective. More often than not this is the case. However, sometimes during the *viva voce* examination which is also conducted before granting the admission into any research programme, the research or admission committee comes up with different suggestions or asks for modification or helps the candidate to look at the research problem from a different perspective which leads to the modification in the research problem. That is why at the stage of proposal; basically research problem is tentative or working.

Hypothesis in Research Proposal

The tentative answer or explanation or guessed solution that the researcher provides for the research question or problem can be best described as working or provisional hypothesis. As the research progresses hypothesis also changes.

Limitations and Delimitations of the Study

Since the prospective researcher is taken for granted as qualifiedly read enough to think about carrying out research, it is expected from him to discuss the limitations and scope of his study. The purpose here is to make him realize the importance of specificity in research process. As research degrees are time bound, the researcher cannot choose something that cannot be done in the allotted period. Time, money, personnel amongst other things ought to be taken into consideration in research. And the things that limit or demarcate the research must be mentioned in the research proposal.

Definition of Terminology

We know the importance of language and terminology. The explanation of the terms and words that are typical of the area in which a candidate wishes to undertake research must be clearly mentioned in the research proposal. This helps the research committee to understand fully what the prospective researcher wants to do and how it can be of any use.

Significance of the Study

This is the section that deals with why the prospective researcher wants to carry out research, how his research can be taken as any contribution to knowledge? This section also covers what the prospective researcher proposes to do, how he will carry out his research, what methodology he is going to adopt to carry out his research?

Review/Survey of Related Literature

Whatever the prospective researcher mentioned up till now in the proposal is solely based on his survey or review of the literature. This review of literature is neither complete nor comprehensive but it helps the researcher formulate the research topic, problem, question and hypothesis, etc. Though it is a provisional review of literature, it assumes an important place in proposal.

Time Schedule

The prospective researcher must mention in research proposal the length of time that the research may take. Many universities set limits to the length of time including extensions in which the research report or thesis must be submitted. However, in research proposal the prospective researcher can specify time schedule by giving an expected break-up of how much time the researcher has allotted to carry out each component of research. This shall give an idea to the research committee that the prospective researcher is very organised and systematic for he has also worked out the time schedule. Nevertheless, everybody knows that it becomes extremely difficult sometimes to stick to the time schedule in research, but by and large it helps carrying out research in time. For even if time overlapping takes place in some cases the researcher tries to constrict some elements which are not that important and give ample time to those that are important. As the research progresses the researcher automatically does this. And after all, this time schedule that is submitted in the proposal is also tentative in nature. As other components of research get modified, time schedule also gets modified.

Budget

If the research involves expenses then the budget requirement for carrying out research must be worked out, and presented to the university. However, if the researcher is going to get the grant from University irrespective of the nature of research that he is undertaking, it is not required to be mentioned in the research proposal. But where there is some spending and the researcher feels that he cannot manage with the grant that he gets, he can submit a proposal. It is always good that in such case he must consult those researchers who have already got such grants and make the proposal properly. Every university has its own system, therefore, if the researcher finds out how the budget proposal should be made in accordance with the university norms it will do really good to him and he will stand a better chance of getting the financial assistance.

Bibliography

The research proposal must have the list of the work consulted for getting the idea to carry out the research and for preparing the proposal. It should be presented in a standard documentation format either, MLA or APA or any other generally accepted format.

QUESTIONS

1. Sketch a research design for your research.
2. How to conceive a research design in literary/language research?
3. What is research problem? Formulate a research problem for your research.
4. What is the difference between finding a problem and formulating a problem?

5. What is research question? Formulate at least 10 questions whose answer you proposed to find in your enquiry.
6. What is Hypothesis? Devise a hypothesis for your enquiry.
7. Discuss different types of hypothesis.
8. Bring out in your topic of enquiry the differences amongst research aim, research question, research problem and research hypothesis.

4

Conducting Research

CONDUCTING RESEARCH

Before a potential researcher sets out to conduct his research, he must prepare a list of all experts who are connected with the subject such as, teachers, scholars, librarians, etc. Some of these people are extremely busy; therefore when the researcher gets their appointment, he must not waste their time by asking useless or frivolous questions. Rather a researcher must go prepared to them carrying questions which are relevant to his research and try to make the most of the time allotted to him for the interview or conversation that he will have with them. He must always carry a letter of request from his supervisor or the department or the university when he seeks experts' appointment and when he meets them. A list of questions must always be with the researcher which he must rehearse before hand, so that only the relevant questions can be posed to experts. Some experts do not like the question list or questionnaire taken out before them. If they are academicians, they may not mind but people from other fields do mind certain things and at times feel a bit irate or threatened. Therefore, the researcher must make his questions appear spontaneous (which of course he has come prepared). If the time is passing and the researcher feels that he got stuck with little or no information about a particular question then he can very politely pose the next question. However, he must make it appear as if it is just a request and he is soliciting information and advice. In reality also, this is the stage of receiving advice and counsel for the researcher.

The researcher must never hand over any questionnaire to the experts. Most of these experts do not like answering questionnaire, unless they are of the researcher's age. If they are senior or holding some big positions they feel disturbed with such things. This is the initial stage. A researcher must remember that he is not into the thick of his research; he is just soliciting information from different experts as to how he could go about his research.

Mostly, people like giving advice. It is always better that the researcher first introduce himself, his topic and his research and what he intends to do. This facilitates the matter for the expert to suggest what the researcher can do, where he can get the literature on the topic or sometimes he may put the researcher to the real person who is an expert in that field. Once the researcher realizes that he got the relevant information, he must thank the expert and take leave. It is also advisable that he writes a letter or sends an email or just leave a note of thank. This will certainly come handy in future should he require the services of the same expert. Acknowledgements of such kinds will always enhance researcher's work etiquette.

Appropriate Stationery

Before embarking on research the researcher needs to buy all appropriate items of stationery that may be required for carrying out research. Some of the items that the researcher may require are: files, boxes, pencils, erasers, pens, notebooks, letters, lose papers, cupboards, computer, printer, appropriate softwares, appropriate word processors, staplers, pins, threads, rulers, video cameras, recorders, etc.

Research Diary

The prospective researcher needs to keep a research diary. This diary must tell him what he should do on what day. He needs to allow for contingencies also in his scheduling that he does in the diary. Research diary is of great help and it reminds the researcher what he did and what he did not do. It is in reality a kind of a map of research; a plan in execution and a plan for execution. It makes researcher time conscious and helps him finish his work in time. It is all about organisation and management.

Checklist

Once he gathered all the relevant information the researcher must prepare a checklist of things that he should do. This checklist must carry the task and the items required for the completion of that task on a day-to-day basis. If a particular task is left undone in a given day it should be done as early as possible. The research dairy must make note of it. And a heading 'tasks unaccomplished' must be given and all those things that are left incomplete must be placed under this section. A researcher is required to see this section daily as priority before he takes up any task that day.

FROM THE SCRATCH: CONDUCTING RESEARCH

The researcher must begin his research from the scratch. He must have read literature while preparing for his research proposal. This can be a pointer in directing him what he should do and where should he begin. However, after getting the seat in doctoral or any research programme he formally begins his research. Therefore, he must begin again from scratch. That is, he must explore the literature, methodologies, etc. that can help him achieve his objective satisfactorily. There are few tasks listed below that he must carry out:

- Literature exploration
- Record keeping
- Reading the literature critically
- Making notes
- Referencing and compiling a bibliography

Literature Exploration

Literature exploration is literature searching. It is the route to all sources of published, printed, aired or broadcast information. Searching the literature helps to increase knowledge and understanding of the topic under investigation. It also helps in identifying different approaches methods and analyses. The information gathered through literature exploration is mostly secondary irrespective of it being textual, statistical, diagrammatic, electronic, visual or auditory. The basic sources for literature searching are: paper-based and electronic. Books, journals, periodicals, abstracts, indexes, directories, research reports, conference papers, market reports, annual reports, organisations' internal records, newspapers, and magazines are paper-based or printed sources. On-line databases, Internet, off-line databases (CD-ROMs), audios, videos and broadcasts are electronic sources.

Record Keeping

It refers to setting down on paper or notebook or index card or in a word processor information about articles, journals, books, records, or any sort of information that is accessed and read by the researcher.

Whatever the system the researcher employs to access information whether index or notebook or word processor, he must record the following information about the text or book or article that he read. They are: (1) the title of the book, or article; (2) the full name of the author/compiler/editor/translator; (3) the year of publication; (4) edition number; (5) revision number if the book is revised; (6) volume no.; (7) place of publication; (8) library or place where the book is found; (9) library catalogue No.; (10) ISBN; (11) Call No.; (12) details where the book is found in which shelf, room, and floor of the library, etc.

As it is the first phase of gathering information, most of the things that go in the record keeping may not be relevant for the final thesis that the researcher is going to submit. But remember this is the initial stage. The shortest time that any University allows for the completion of doctoral research and submission is about two years. And in that period the researcher would realize that he would forget very many things. So finally when cross referencing, checking, or quoting any source takes place and if the book, article is not found then there will a problem. Therefore, any item of information may come handy at the end which will ease research tension and facilitate the work. Additionally, it is a time saving technique. Therefore, sometimes record keeping looks very boring, tiresome and taxing, nevertheless it must be carried out to avoid all kinds of research snags and flaws that show up while the research is in progress.

Reading the Material Critically

Reading becomes fruitful when it is assimilated critically. Critical reading refers to the understanding of the text in its right context. Once the text is understood, the job of the researcher is to find out what are the elements in the text that are related with his research. How it shall be of any help to him or to the readers? The text can be anything from dissertation to a single line statement. However, before the text is chosen the research scholar must be quick to find out whether the text is worth reading for his research. If it is then he can spend time on it. Therefore, the reading technique of effective skimming will be of great help. The researcher must first gain the overview of the text. The best way is to begin with the title of the text. Title offers lots of answers to the curiosity about the worthiness of the text (in relation to the research). Title page often gives information about the subject, the methodology or approach, the name of the author, the year of publication and the publisher also. The second thing that the researcher-reader must do is, reading the 'table of content' which gives him a very comprehensive outline about the book, and the main topics and subtopics that the text deals with. Next the researcher must read the 'preface', in case of dissertations and research papers 'abstract'. This area illuminates the intention and purpose behind the writing of the text. It also provides particularly in case of dissertations and theses in language research, the summary of the findings of research. This helps the researcher immensely to establish or disestablish the connection between the text and his research. Then, he must spend some time with the index, references, glossary sections, etc. These sections throw light on the very process through which information is gathered and explanation is made. If the work is of seminal kind then it necessitates reading all the chapters particularly the introduction and conclusion so that the researcher can decide about the substantive nature of the text and relate or break it with his research, etc. If the text or any part of it is useful then the researcher can take up a detailed reading, but he must always try to relate it with his research. There are few basic things that he can do once he decided to read the text. It is always important to prepare a reading schedule. Whichever part of the day or night suits the researcher he must use it efficiently to make an effective and meaningful reading. He must divide reading into time periods or manageable sections of the text. Suppose the researcher decides that he shall read for three hours a day, then he can divide these three hours in three stretches of one hour each. If the researcher decides that he should go through at least 120 pages a day, he can divide it in three sessions each session should carry 40 page reading. Likewise, chapter-wise, and topic-wise, reading can be done. Some people feel comfortable making notes as they read and some people make notes after completion of a section. Some researcher holds that making notes while reading obstructs or interferes the concentration. My personal advise to the researcher is to keep always a pencil and an eraser and if the text is his own then he can underline the points that he wants to make notes of, and if it is borrowed from the library then a small opening and closing bracket or a small dot can be put on either side of the margin of the text which can be copied down once the reading is completed [though technically it can also be taken as violation of the copyrights, in a sense that it may be construed that the book has been damaged].

Making Notes

Making notes involves recording the chapter headings, summary, statements, words, expressions, terms, opinions, etc. In other words, anything that the researcher feels that can be of use to his research he must make notes of it. Notes can be recorded at the back of the index card, in the notebooks, or loose sheets of paper, etc.

REVIEW OF LITERATURE

Literature review is a writing that carries past and current study of a particular subject. It is taken up to carry critical points about the previous works on a topic. However, the word 'critical' here refers to significantly unbiased study and statement about the previous works.

Every researcher needs to go through a large chunk of literature before he decides to undertake research. The reading of literature or related literature on the topic under investigation happens at three obvious stages: first before drafting research proposal; second, after getting admission at the initial stage of conducting research and third all through the research till the completion of the thesis. The first stage is pretty apparent, unless the prospective researcher reads the literature he cannot come up with any topic or area to undertake research. At this stage either the prospective researcher's own interest or the prospective researcher's teacher's suggestions and guidance or just through reading the researcher comes across a problem area where research can be conducted and some contribution to knowledge can be made. Here the prospective researcher may read several articles, books, journals, etc. All of these are cited in the prospective researcher's proposal. The second time he reviews or surveys literature is when he gets the admission in the University and he undertakes research literally. This is the first and initial stage of conducting real research. At this stage, he may collect the information pertaining to his topic and read whatever is available on his topic or related with his topic. This stage is crucial for the researcher at this stage tries to formulate the real research problem, hypothesis and aim of his research. Whatever he submitted in his research proposal may begin getting modified from here onwards. Because the researcher may find a new problem which in reality may require more attention, or he may find that the problem that he mentioned has been mostly covered by some other researchers and there is not pretty much that he can do, so on and so forth. Thus, whatever he collects at this stage, most of it he notes down to present it in his thesis. The third time that the researcher undertakes reviewing of literature is throughout the research. That is, after finishing the initial reading and setting that down, when he undertakes research literally, that is, when the researcher is doing field work, choosing right methodology, choosing appropriate method, collecting data and finally writing thesis. During all these phases the researcher reads literature available on these topics and his topic of investigation. Thus, these are the three stages of reviewing or surveying of literature which are interrelated and interconnected with one another.

Literature review involves two components with respect to its coverage: subject and time. That is, every literature review involves discussion of a subject in a particular period of time. Literature review traces the intellectual development made in a subject over a period of time. Or, it connects the intellectual development of the past to the present and seeks its future direction.

One of the purposes of literature review in dissertations is to demonstrate to the examiners, scholars and readers, the notions, ideas, principles, methodologies, or knowledge which has been developed by accredited scholars and experts on a topic undertaken for investigation. Literature review is determined by the objective, the problem, the hypothesis of research; though surprisingly in many researches it is literature review that helps in identifying objective of research, formulating research question and speculating hypothesis.

Besides expanding knowledge and increasing understanding about the topic under investigation, writing a literature review helps the researcher gain skills in seeking information and making critical appraisal.

Literature review most importantly identifies areas of controversy in literature, which are unresolved or are unsettled.

Literature review is a written synopsis of the findings from the literature exploration undertaken by the researcher. It is written to prove that the researcher possesses intellectual depth and has made a substantive investigation of the books, articles, etc. related to the topic he has undertaken for investigation. The researcher is expected to provide a scholarly and critical analysis of the works attempted before him. Most scholars believe that literature review must not be just a descriptive summary of the works. Rather, it must be written around themes and ideas. It must involve comparison between different works on the same topic by different authors or researchers. It should involve evaluation of the works which can be done by pointing out the weaknesses and strengths of different works and it must be always written bearing in mind the study and the nature of the study undertaken.

Literature Review Format and Type

Any piece of composition can be set into three parts: introduction, body and conclusion, so also literature review. More than the format of literature review, it is the type that receives attention from the examiners of the dissertations. There are several types of literature review mentioned below, but the student of humanities are advised to go for the compare-contrast, analytical or evaluative type as they help students to improve their power of critical and constructive understanding and appreciation of their own research work.

Chronological Type Literature Review

This is the most popular type of literature review. It follows time in sequence. That is the literature that the researcher gathered is presented in 'the literature review' section according to its date of writing or publishing: from the earliest work (written or published on the topic under investigation) to the latest. For example, if somebody is working on 'language universals', he is supposed to present the first treatise written (or that he found to be the earliest one, date-wise) on the topic first and moves on to the latest treatise on that topic. In other words the division of the chronological type review of literature is done date-wise. Nevertheless, what information the researcher provides in his presentation about the topic solely depends on the researcher. He sometimes just presents the summary of the work without making any observation on the topic. This becomes often descriptive and its connection with the researcher's own topic may be just the shared or identical areas of investigation. Nothing goes beyond that. Most of the examiners of the dissertations do not like this type particularly in literary and language research. Exception can be made in case of history research. Nevertheless, this type of review can be made really substantive if the researcher takes the trouble of maintaining date-wise introduction of the research work that he found and try to assess and evaluate it with respect to his own research.

Topic-wise Type Literature Review

Some supervisors advise their research participants to divide their literature review topic-wise. For example, if the research topic is 'language universals' and the researcher is focusing on areas like, phonetic similarities, structural similarities, names similarities, etc. then he should present his review of books, articles, etc. accordingly under these topics. Under phonetic similarities, he will present the works connected with phonetics, under structural similarities he shall present his review of the works associated with the structure of languages, and under names similarities he will present the work that he read on names that are similar in different languages of the world. This type of literature review is good, and it suits literature and language research provided it is analytical and evaluative.

Compare-Contrast Type Literature Review

In this type the researcher attempts to compare and contrast works of different authors from one another and then with the work that the researcher himself has undertaken. The writing style could be descriptive, analytical, argumentative, anything, but the emphasis will be placed on the differences and similarities amongst the works under review.

Methodological Type Literature Review

This type does not involve the description analysis or interpretation of the content of the books or articles, rather it deals with the methods or research designs of the researchers or authors.

There are no hard and fast rules as to what approach or what type a research scholar employs to present the review of literature in his dissertation. The classification of review of literature can be done with different types of writing style. Like, analytical, descriptive, evaluative, cause-effect, summarizing, etc. However, if any of the types mentioned above is followed, the research shall look systematic and well organised.

There is no denying that there shall be overlap of these three types discussed above, namely, chronological, topic-wise, and compare-contrast. For instance, a researcher can have a chronological format, but in that format he presents his review of books topic-wise, and additionally if he compares, contrasts, analyses and evaluates different works, his review shall be more substantive and effective.

A researcher needs to decide which type of reviewing of literature is best suited to his research. For that he needs to first pose few questions to himself about his research, like what is the nature of his research: exploratory, explanatory, applied, etc.? What are the problems or issues he wishes to undertake and to whom they relate? For example, are the issues connected with theory, or methodology, or methods? Is the research quantitative or qualitative, etc.? When the answers to these questions are found then it becomes very easy for the researcher to start writing literature review. But for all these he is supposed to read a lot. And on top of these the researcher is also supposed to know how many sources should he use? What must be the criterion to use sources? Should he use all sources in his review for example, books, articles, magazines, websites, audio videos, CD, DVD?, etc. Or should he just go for one source? For example, the review is based on only dissertations or peer-reviewed articles, etc. Whatever the researcher does, if he makes it apparent in his introduction to the section on reviewing of literature it will be well received and sometimes appreciated for its specificity.

When reviewing a book or article or thesis, the researcher is required to gather at least the following pieces of information:

- What is the problem or issue?
- What is the hypothesis?
- What is the author's methodological approach or the theoretical framework?
- What is the research design?
- What is the nature of the study, i.e. exploratory, descriptive, explanatory applied action?
- What are the findings of the author?

- And how the work of the author is related with the researcher's topic under investigation?

Remember, the purpose to write literature review is just not to summarize whatever is written in the past, but to present the knowledge or information gathered, by interpreting, re-interpreting and connecting it to the work under investigation (i.e., the researcher's study).

DOCUMENTATION

Any text, write-up, video, audio, etc. that explains some features, characteristics of an object, phenomenon, and system can be called documentation. But in research, documentation just does not refer to any material recorded but also it is an act and manifestation of collation, coding, and synopsizing of printed material for present and future reference. Documentation in research is a piece of information that verifies and confirms whether something is true or not. It is an act of validating the fact and truth. And documenting source in research refers to the act of acknowledging through citing in text or in bibliography the work that a researcher has used to advance and further his research.

Documenting sources is indispensable in every research. It is the sincere acknowledgement of the researcher about the investigation carried out by the previous scholars and researchers. This acknowledgement is necessitated by academic honesty. No student is fit to consider himself a researcher if he does not acknowledge the contribution of the previous scholars and masters in his area of investigation. And the art of acknowledging the contribution of the previous scholars by citing their names, their work titles and the nature of their contribution in reality is what documentation is all about.

Citation of statements and quotations with complete information is required in every research project report and thesis. However, in this section I would like to discuss more of how we can document a source, than why we should document a source? There are several traditionally frozen styles that have developed over the past few years for citing sources. But the most powerful and widely followed styles are MLA and APA styles. MLA style is developed by the Modern Language Association of America. And APA style is developed by American Psychological Association. Most scholars in humanities either follow MLA or APA. However, as long as there is consistency and coherence, any style can be adopted. Nevertheless, other styles have been developed alongside which are as good as these styles. The purpose behind all these styles is to facilitate the research work reading. Some universities, institutions, and journals and in some cases even the publishers set norms in this regard. They demand that the citing of source must be done in a particular style. Thus, before documenting sources the researcher must know any such guide line available from his respective university. In some cases the supervisors or guides demand of a particular style adoption. Here also researcher must be careful whatever the supervisor demands he must produce his writing in that style. If the university, the research supervisor or research committee does not insist on any particular style, a researcher can develop his own style. However, the ways and the terminology that he uses must be clearly specified for the understanding of the examiners and the readers. The most important thing in citation is giving all the details about the text: author, title, publication agency, year of publication, place of publication, page numbers, volume numbers, revision, reprint, etc.

Documenting Sources

We shall discuss and have some samples of different citation styles. A research scholar must have different referencing style books and guides with him when he writes his thesis. Given below are samples from MLA, APA styles and some other styles; but for the complete assimilation of these styles the researcher is advised to go through books available on these styles like *MLA Handbook for Writers of Research Papers* (Joseph Gibaldi, sixth edition, 2004), etc.

MLA in-Text Citations

In MLA documentation style in-text citation refers to the acknowledgement of the source in the text of the research or thesis paper. This is done through presenting parenthetical citations which are keyed to the bibliography or references, or alphabetical list of works cited that appears at the end of the thesis or paper. For Example:

In-Text Citation

The two pillars upon which a theory of criticism must rest are an account of value and an account of communication (Richards 20).

Here the parenthetical citation (Richards 20) suggests that the information is taken from the work of an author by name Richard and the information can be found on page 20. This is keyed to bibliography or works-cited list where complete name of the author, the title of the work, its publication place, its publisher's name and its year of publication are found in the following manner:

In the References

Richards, Ivor Armstrong. *Principles of Literary Criticism.* London: Routledge & Kegan Paul, 1924.

APA in-Text Citation

Same example can be taken to present the difference between MLA and APA. In APA, the in-text citation is presented in the following manner: (Richards, 1924, p. 20). It is mostly held that since the time-consciousness is crucial to any research in sciences, thus the year of research is also presented in parenthetical citation in APA, which is keyed to bibliographic section or works-cited list, where the complete information about the source can be found in the following manner:

In the References

Richards, I.A. (1924) *Principles of Literary Criticism,* London: Routledge & Kegan Paul.

The Differences

The examples above present some differences between MLA and APA documentation styles. First, in MLA style the author's name appears full that is without any initials, whereas in APA the author's name carries initials, the last name is written first. Second, in MLA style the title of the work is underlined, whereas it is italicised in APA style. Third, all the first letters of the content words in the title are capitalized in the MLA style, whereas only the first letter of the first word is capitalized in the APA style. Third, the year of publication comes last in MLA style, whereas it comes next to the name of the author in the APA style. Fourth, in MLA style the year of publication is not bracketed, whereas it is put in brackets in APA style. However, in both the styles the first line of the entry is flush with the left margin and the following lines are indented.

The CSE/CBE Style

The Council of Science Editors (CSE) which was formerly called The Council of Biology Editors (CBE) is a scientific style of documentation. It present two approaches for documenting sources: (1) a citation/sequence system, and (2) a name/year system. In this style of citation the term *References* is specifically used as it does not give any information other than what is cited in the text of the paper or thesis.

The CSE/CBE Citation-Sequence System

The citation/sequence in-text citation system depends on numbers. It does not give any parenthetical information. It employs a superscripted number at the end of a clause or sentence or paragraph identifying the content in it as outside source material. This superscripted number is keyed or referred to a correspondingly numbered entry in the references list or works-cited list at the end of the paper or thesis or book. If a reference is referred multiple times, the superscripted number in each case will be the same. It must be borne in mind that the superscripted number appears after the punctuation mark in the text and there is no space between punctuation mark and the superscripted number.

Example

In-Text Citation

The two pillars upon which a theory of criticism must rest are an account of value and an account of communication.[1]

In the References

[1.] Richards, I.A. Principles of Literary Criticism. London: Routledge & Kegan Paul; 1924. 283 p.

In this citation style spaces are used after colon and semicolon separating city, publisher, date and total pages. Note that semi colon is used after the publisher's name and the total number of pages that the book comprises, is given after the year of publication and small p. is placed at the end of the reference.

The CSE/CBE Name-Year System

The name-year citation style contains the name of the author and the date of publication at the point of reference just like, MLA and APA styles of citation. It is keyed with the references list at the end.

Example

In-Text Citation

Richards (1924, p. 20) says that the two pillars upon which a theory of criticism must rest are an account of value and an account of communication.

In the References

1. Richards, I.A. Principles of Literary Criticism. London: Routledge & Kegan Paul; 1924. 283 p.

In the references list both styles i.e. citation-sequence and name-year are written the same way. Except in the name-year style it is the entry number which is determined by alphabetical order, whereas in the citation-sequence it is the superscripted number which takes the entry number's place.

Chicago-Turabian Documentation

In this citation style the superscript is used right after the completion of the quotation, just like CBE/CSE citation. However the citation is keyed or referred to the notes at the bottom of the page or at the end of the paper which are traditionally called footnote or endnote. The notes at the bottom of the page are separated from text with a typed line, 1.5 inches long. In case of endnotes the title is not *References* as in CBE/CSE style citation, but it is *Notes*. In the footnote or endnote the same number is used without superscript. The entry in the notes or reference list will be indented for five spaces. A full stop or period is used after the number and two spaces between the number and the name of the author.

Example

In-Text Citation

The two pillars upon which a theory of criticism must rest are an account of value and an account of communication.[1]

In the Notes (References)

The sample entry in the *notes* will appear in like the following way:

1. Richards, Ivor Armstrong, *Principles of Literary Criticism* (London: Routledge & Kegan Paul, 1924), 20.

In this referencing style the city of publication, publishers, and the year of publication are bracketed and the page number is placed outside the bracket without any p. or pp. abbreviation for pages.

Harvard Referencing Style

Harvard Referencing style is also very similar to the APA style in in-text citation. It is an author-year citation style. If the researcher is using the quotation then the citation comes initially in the sentence, with the page number from where the statement is quoted.

Examples

In-Text Citation

The two pillars upon which a theory of criticism must rest are an account of value and an account of communication (Richards 1924).

Richard (1924: 20) says: 'The two pillars upon which a theory of criticism must rest are an account of value and an account of communication.'

In the References

Richards I.A. 1924. *Principles of Literary Criticism.* London: Routledge & Kegan Paul.

Vancouver Referencing Style

This style is commonly used in medical and scientific journals. The reference list appears at the end of the article or book. The entries appear in the references in the same order that they have been cited in the text. The bibliography is always presented as a separate list which is arranged either author-wise or title-wise alphabetically. In this style in-text citation is done through numbers. Arabic numerals in square or round brackets or in superscripts are used after the quotation. The number is used even if the author's name is used in the text. The original number assigned to the reference is used if that reference is cited multiple times.

Example

In-Text Citation

Richard says: 'The two pillars upon which a theory of criticism must rest are an account of value and an account of communication.'(1)

The two pillars upon which a theory of criticism must rest are an account of value and an account of communication.[1]

In the References

Richards I.A. Principles of literary criticism. London: Routledge & Kegan Paul; 1924.

Oxford System or Documentary-Note System

In this system the in-text citation uses superscript at the end of the sentence. It is keyed or referred to footnote at the bottom of the page or endnote at the end of the paper or thesis. However, a separate bibliography where the list of all the works-cited and the works consulted is also given.

Example

In-Text Citation

Quoting

Richards notes: 'The two pillars upon which a theory of criticism must rest are an account of value and an account of communication.'[1]

Summarising and Paraphrasing

Richards notes that the two pillars upon which a theory of criticism must rest are an account of value and an account of communication.[1]

In the References (Footnote, Endnote)

I.A. Richards, *Principles of Literary Criticism*, Routledge & Kegan Paul, London, 1924, p. 20.

Note that in this referencing style the initials of the name are placed, and then the last name of the author is given. Another marked difference in this style of referencing is, the name of the publisher is written first then the city of publication.

All the examples given above for in-text citation and referencing are conventionalised and are perfectly acceptable all around the world. However, teachers, guides, supervisors, instructors and professionals of different subjects prefer different styles and insist their students or research participants to choose a particular style. Nonetheless, it is always advisable for the research participant to know these styles. In case the supervisor gives the freedom to choose the referencing style to the researcher then the researcher must compare and contrast the effectiveness of these styles and their fit with his research work and select the style. If the researcher feels that he can develop his own style he can do that but for the readers and examiners he must offer guidelines to follow his own style and prove its logicality and reasonableness for why it is required. Another important point that the researcher must bear in mind whatever style he uses he must be consistent and coherent in it. In most of the style guides in the introduction or in the preface it is clearly mentioned that for which subject or stream the style in question is suitable. This helps the researcher to decide which style he should go for.

I have just given one example of in-text citation and referencing. That is of single author, first edition, etc. For the work of more than one author, or for journal, or encyclopaedia citation or reference the researcher is advised to go through the following guides so that a comprehensive understanding and assimilation of the style can be made and employed in the research work:

Marie Gaspar and Meron Shepherd, Geelong (2005) *Guide to assignment writing and referencing.* Vic.: Deakin University.

Style manual for authors, editors and printers. Canberra: Australian Govt. Pub. Service 2002, 6th ed.

Xia Li, Medford, (1996) *Electronic styles: A handbook for citing electronic information*, 2nd ed. NJ: Information Today.

Janice R. Walker & Todd Taylor, (c1998). *The Columbia guide to online style*, New York: Columbia University Press.

Andrew Harnack, Eugene Kleppinger, (c1998) *Online! A reference guide to using Internet sources.* New York: St. Martin's Press.

The Chicago manual of style, Chicago: University of Chicago Press, 2003. 15th ed.

Publication Manual of the American Psychological Association. Washington, DC: American Psychological Association, 2001. 5th ed.

Carol J. Amato, Corona, (c2002) The world's easiest guide to using the APA: a user-friendly manual for formatting research papers according to the American Psychological Association style guide. 3rd ed., Calif: Stargazer Pub. Co.

Joseph Gibaldi, (1998) *MLA style manual and guide to scholarly publishing*, 2nd ed. New York: Modern Language Association of America.

Joseph Gibaldi, (2004) *MLA Handbook for Writers of Research Papers*, 6th ed., First East-West Press ed. New Delhi: East-West Press Pvt. Ltd.

The Oxford style manual, (2003) edited and compiled by Robert Ritter, Oxford: Oxford University Press.

Referencing using Vancouver style, Academic skills, Deakin University.

Style manual for authors, editors and printers, 2002, 6th ed., revised by Snooks & Co. Qld: John Wiley & Sons.

Janice R. Walker and Todd Taylor, (c1998) *The Columbia guide to online style*, New York: Columbia University Press.

QUESTIONS

1. What are the prerequisite for conducting research?
2. What does critical reading mean and how it is undertaken?

3. What is literature review? Discuss its various types.
4. Which type of literature review you wish to adopt for your study and why?
5. What is documentation?
6. Discuss the chief characteristics of MLA citation style.
7. Discuss the chief characteristics of APA citation style.
8. Discuss the difference between citation-sequence system and name-year system of referencing.

5

Crafting the Thesis

THE THESIS

Thesis is a report of research and investigation that a candidate undertakes. This report mostly carries the statement about 'what is discovered or invented?' However, with the passage of time and for the confirmation of the thing discovered or invented, the researcher was required to also make a statement or report 'how it is discovered or invented?' In the past, universities did not distribute doctoral degrees when a thesis was submitted. The process of entitlement to doctoral degree was disputation. This process has survived to this day also in the form of viva voce examination. However, how thesis came into its present form and what was its origin were the questions that Almack (2006: 4-5) investigated succinctly. He writes:

> Universities, in their genesis, were similar in their organisation to the corporations of workingmen and the commercial and trade leagues with which they were contemporaneous. The University was, after the guild model, an association for taking apprentices into the arts, developing them into journeymen, and at length admitting them into the teaching crafts as masters. The essential outcome of the instruction given the student was skill in disputation.
>
> Therefore, after the prospective master had passed his preliminary tests and given instruction under the supervision of a certified teacher, he was permitted to present himself for examination for admission to the

> highest rank. The examination took the form of a disputation upon some proposition which the student offered as his "thesis", with the applicant contender against all comers....
>
> The disputation as a test for the degree continued for over five hundred years. At the commencement at Harvard, in 1759, after the salutatory, there followed a syllogistic disputation in Latin, in which four or five or more of those who were distinguished as scholars in the class were appointed by the president as respondents, and to whom were assigned certain questions which the respondents maintained, while the remainder of the class severely opposed and endeavoured to invalidate the arguments presented. This disputation was conducted wholly in Latin, and in the form of syllogism and thesis. (C.F. Birdseye, *Individual Training in Our Colleges*, p. 61)

This practice of conferring of degree on the basis of disputation was found in German British Universities also; University of Edinburgh had also some such similar practice. But this practice fell gradually, because of the introduction of printing which paved way for written thesis. Noting this aspect Almack (2006: 7-9) observes:

> The introduction of printing was a decided stimulus to the development of the written thesis. New fields of study brought new thesis subjects into use. At Harvard, in 1640, an applicant for the "second degree" was required to 'give up a system, or synopsis, or sum of logic, philosophy, arithmetic, geometry, or astronomy'. A Cambridge student wrote, in 1710: 'I have a very little time to spare at present, for I am preparing a thesis...being to come up ye beginning of May'; and by 1761, the regulations specified that candidates for degrees "read their theses before the moderators," with the understanding that the best were to be published by the university.

> ...after the founding of the university of Berlin (1809) a new type of thesis was created a type designed to set the academic thesis-pattern for a long time to come.
>
> ...the master of arts degree still retained much of its old significance—competence to teach; the master of science degree indicated the ability in research; the doctor's degree stood for accomplishment in the ultimate essentials of research—ability to make original contribution to knowledge.

The Evolution of Thesis

Thesis is an intellectual proposition or statement presented in written or electronic form as a contribution to the field of knowledge to receive some traditional academic recognition. This proposition or statement is made after thorough research and investigation of or in any field of knowledge.

Almack (2006: 10-11) notes: "originally thesis meant a proposition which the student proposed to defend, as when, in 1762, a student at Cambridge as his thesis 'affirmed the justice of hell torments and capital punishment'. Taken literally, thesis signifies 'a thing laid down, a statement, a proposition; specifically, a position or proposition which a person advances and offers to maintain'."

A second stage in academic progress was reached when university teachers realizing the futility of scholastic debate came to hold that a thesis should represent a field of knowledge to be investigated. This group at some time claimed that investigation without comment and conclusion should be presented as the comment and conclusion sometimes invalidate the results. Thus thesis was only constituted of the data. However, to-day thesis is commonly regarded as a coherent report of research in which both the process and the results are given. Its origin is a problem and its central proposition is hypothesis (Almack, 2006: 10-11).

The trends in research of late have widely differed from what they were few years ago. The emphasis is on the contribution to the field of knowledge. Simply reading of the subject matter or any field and its understanding is not considered to be 'contribution'. Rather, it is considered 'contribution' when the candidate studies any given field, finds problem in it, and solves it. In some cases even identification of the problem itself is considered to be a great discovery and contribution to the field of knowledge. Thus, research in reality involves study of the problem to solve it, and the written or electronic statement of it, is presented in the thesis.

The purpose behind giving the history of thesis writing is to make a research scholar equipped the way doctoral degrees evolved. The way they came into being. Nowadays in some universities particularly in scientific fields the very dissertation or thesis is taken to be traditional. And instead the vogue is to ask the students to submit four or five publishable research papers to be entitled to receive doctoral degree. Nevertheless, the traditional thesis submission is still the most popular way with the research scholars.

Thesis and the Concept of Contribution to Knowledge

Since it is believed that every research must be a contribution to knowledge, then how can it be determined whether a research work has made any contribution to knowledge or not? Almack (2006: 38) reports one incident which throws light on the concept of contribution to knowledge. He writes:

> A few years ago, a student in one of our large universities submitted his completed thesis to the graduate council. The council refused to accept it on the grounds that it was not a contribution to knowledge. In defending the thesis, the student contended that a contribution to knowledge may be made by: (1) adding new facts and principles, (2) adding new techniques, and (3) by making available to the many what was before available only to the few. His thesis, he felt measured up to the third criterion; but the council refused to accept the validity of the third principle.

Undoubtedly, even the third criterion that he suggested can be taken as valid on the grounds that it can be placed under dissemination of knowledge. And research is just not about contribution but also about diffusion of knowledge. The thesis subjects hinges on the concept of contribution. They can be, discovering facts and phenomena about some issues; discovering new principles and laws in any subject; discovering new courses, methods, designs, techniques, and skills in any subject; making new inferences from the earlier studies; adding new facts, adding new techniques; attempting new understanding of the live issues; inventing anything that helps improve the condition and state of any object, fact, experience, practice and understanding; investigation undertaken to study the authenticity of any proposition, book or object, etc.

PhD THESIS MODELS

Knowledge explosion, creativity and search for novelty necessitated the change in PhD thesis models. The thesis models differ from subject to subject. Science and technology not only enhanced the process of writing and facilitated documentation but also opened up several ways in which the thesis can be packaged. I remember one of the external examiners of my PhD observed that I should have presented the data in Compact Disc instead of incorporating it in printed versions in my thesis that made my thesis very voluminous. The observation made me think and speculate that in future, we may be asked to submit thesis in CDs/DVDs, etc. There is also a great possibility that the Universities demand a movie being made of the research and submitted.

However, as long as Universities demand that the thesis be written, we are required to follow some general principles of thesis writing. There are two PhD Models that are prescribed by universities nowadays. They are classical model and taught model.

Dunleavy (2003: 5-6) discusses at length these two types of PhD models. She writes: 'There are two main types of PhD education: the 'classical' model associated closely with a 'big book' type of thesis; and the more modern 'taught PhD model', normally associated with a shorter 'papers model dissertation'.'

The classical model has developed over centuries. It is prevalent in British and European universities. It is widely used in Humanities and Social Sciences. Usually, a supervisor is assigned to the candidate who guides and supervises the candidate to carry out the research and then helps him in producing the thesis. The work is examined by separate examiners who evaluate the work according to the guidelines of the university and declare whether the candidate is fit to be awarded doctoral degree or not.

'Taught PhD model' is relatively new and quite popular particularly in sciences and is practiced in most of the American universities. It involves extensive coursework usually extending over two to three years and assessed at the end by general examination. And submission of quality publishable research papers which are assessed by the PhD or dissertation committee. PhD Committee always includes the student's main adviser plus some faculty members who do not work closely with the student. The main adviser is just like the supervisor or guide of the classical model. The dissertation committee assesses the research papers and conduct the dissertation defence before declaring the student qualified or otherwise (see Dunleavy 6-9).

In India classical model is widely in practice. Most universities provide guidelines as to what type of thesis is required to be submitted. Some even put the limit to the big book model of thesis. It is stipulated by the universities that the thesis must not exceed 350 pages, excluding tables, charts and photos, etc.

However, as some universities offer doctoral courses or programmes in India both at regular and part time basis, the modes of doctoral programme and its requirements are also variegated. Nonetheless, universities' stipulation of the guidelines must be in conformity with the basic stipulations of the University Grant Commission, and then only it is recognised in India.

In addition to the 'classical model' and 'taught PhD model' there are several models that have developed of late. For example, one popular model in India incorporates the features of both taught model and classical model. The students are required to first do the course work where the necessary subjects are taught, then they take the exam, and after passing that exam they start working towards their thesis. The thesis would be made on the lines of classical model thesis. This is a very common practice in India.

THESIS STRUCTURE AND WRITING

Once the research is completed, analysis is done, and the findings are made, the task of setting these in research writing begins. The writing in research is not different from any piece of formal writing style. However, the emphasis is laid on the organisation of the thesis.

There are certain conditions that are conventionalised in research writing. They involve the presentation of research work in a certain format though, it is the finding which is of paramount importance and which is taken to be the contribution to knowledge. However, a researcher as a participant of a university is required to follow the conventions of research presentation in thesis format. And every thesis must carry components such as abstract, content page, background to the study, survey of literature, works-cited list, etc. besides the real research and its findings. The reason behind this is to suggest that a researcher learnt the art of carrying out research in a systematic and acknowledging way. Here the word acknowledgement is very pertinent. For most of the things that the researcher carries in his research involves his direct or indirect acknowledgement of the works undertaken by others in the related or otherwise fields. This is obvious in the survey, citations of the research, etc.

The following is the list of components found in humanities research:

The Division of the Thesis

- Title Page
- Signature Page
- Statement of Ethics Approval (where applicable)
- Dedication (optional)

- Acknowledgements (optional)
- Abstract
- Co-Authorship Statement (where applicable)
- Table of Contents
- List of Tables (where applicable)
- List of Figures (where applicable)
- List of Symbols, Abbreviations, Acronyms, and Nomenclature and the Glossary (where applicable)
- Preface (optional)
- Body of the thesis
    - Introduction Chapter
    - Methodology Chapter
    - Analysis Chapter
    - Findings and Results Chapter
    - Conclusion Chapter
- Bibliography or Work Cited or References
- Appendices

Title Page

Title page of the thesis is the front page which displays important information about the research. It is also a part of front matter or preliminaries of the thesis. It mostly presents three pieces of information: the topic of the research, the name of the researcher and the institution where the research is registered and submitted. Some researchers present the name of the supervisor also on the title page.

Topic of the Research: Research topic can be presented severally. In plain statement form, question form, and explanatory form, etc. However, it must always be borne in mind that the research topic must attract the attention of the reader. It must be an invitation to study. Research topic in reality is the integration of research problem/question and research finding/answer.

The Name of the Researcher: The full name of the researcher must be given on the title page; initials must be avoided, unless the name is written that way all through the researcher's educational life. However, some universities stipulate that it should be given the way it appeared in the masters' programme certificate.

The Name of the University or Institution: The name of University where the researcher registered and where he is required to submit his thesis must also be given on the title page.

The Text on the Title Page: Mostly a text which states for what degree the thesis is written is mentioned, for example, "A Thesis submitted to the Department of English, MANUU in Partial Fulfilment of the Requirements for the Degree of Doctor of Philosophy."

The Date: The month and year of submission must also be given on the title page at the bottom just above the name of the university.

Sample Title Page

Box 5.1

Urdu and English Vowels: A Comparative Study

Syed Mohammed Haseebuddin Quadri

Supervisor
Dr P.V. Dhamija
Professor
Department of Phonetics and Spoken English
CIEFL Hyderabad

A dissertation submitted in partial fulfilment of the requirements for the
Degree of Master of Philosophy in English
(Linguistics and Phonetics)

Central Institute of English and Foreign Languages
Hyderabad
July 1997

Signature Page or Certificate and Declaration Page

Some Universities have signature page which carries the signature of the candidate, supervisor, head of the department and dean, etc. However, in some universities two separate titles, Certificate and Declaration, are used instead of signature paper. Mostly, Certificate is issued by the supervisor stating that the thesis was not submitted for any degree in any other University and the work carried out by the candidate under his/her supervision is completely original. The candidate in the declaration page also states the same that the research work is original and it is not submitted in other university for any degree whatsoever, etc.

Sample Certificate and Declaration Page

Box 5.2: Certificate by the Supervisor

Certificate

This is to certify that the thesis entitled '*English Language Teaching through Distance Education: A Case Study of Dr. B R Ambedkar Open University*' submitted by Mr S. Mohammed Shafiullah for the award of the degree of Master of Philosophy in English to Maulana Azad National Urdu University, Hyderabad, is the original work carried out by him under my supervision. The thesis has not been submitted for any degree, diploma, or other similar titles earlier, and no part of it has been published or sent for the publication at the time of submission.

Signature Supervisor

Date: 2-11-07

Dr Syed Mohammed Haseebuddin Quadri
Reader, Department of English, MANUU

Box 5.3: Declaration/Certificate by the Researcher

Declaration

I hereby declare that the thesis entitled '*English Language Teaching through Distance Education: A Case Study of Dr B.R. Ambedkar Open University*' submitted by me for the award of the degree of Master of Philosophy in English to Maulana Azad National Urdu University, Hyderabad, is the original work carried out by me under the supervision of Dr Syed Mohammed Haseebuddin Quadri, Department of English, Maulana Azad National Urdu University, Hyderabad. The thesis has not been submitted for any degree, diploma, or other similar titles earlier, and no part of it has been published or sent for the publication at the time of submission.

Signature Candidate

Date: 2-11-07

S. Mohammed Shafiullah

Dedication Page

It is an optional page. If the researcher wants to dedicate his work to any person who is close to him or who inspired him or who helped him, he can dedicate the thesis to that person. Mostly, scholars in India dedicate their thesis to their parents. Nevertheless, this page is optional. If it is not included in the thesis the structure of the thesis is not violated. The Dedication page does not carry any headings. It must be as brief as possible.

Acknowledgement Page

The Acknowledgment page must carry the heading 'Acknowledgements'. Though some scholars consider this page to be optional, I feel a researcher must include this page necessarily in his thesis. When a researcher carries out his research there are uncountable number of hurdles he faces but along with these uncountable hurdles and problems he gets equal number of facilities and opportunities to overcome these hurdles and solve his problems. These facilities and opportunities are mainly provided by different people at different occasions. What if these people wouldn't have appeared? How the researcher could have completed his tasks? Etc. The very fact that the researcher has completed his research means that at every step he had been helped by different people and to acknowledge their help should be the top priority of the researcher. These people might be anybody from the researcher's supervisor, father and mother, his wife, his children, his brothers and sisters, his cousins, his friends, his teachers, his colleagues, his servants to any institution or organization, etc. It does not take much, just the mentioning of name makes people happy. And it is the least thing that the researcher can do for them.

Hyland (2004; in Paltridge and Starfield, pp. 160-61) points out that there are typically three stages in Acknowledgement sections: a *reflecting move* which makes some introspective comments on writer's research experience, a *thanking move* which give credit to individuals and institutions, and an *announcing move* which accepts responsibility for any flaws or errors and dedicates the thesis to an individual or individual/s. Of all these, only *thanking move* is obligatory.

These three stages can be understood from a following single example of an Acknowledgement:

> Well! Everybody who carried out research knew what it takes to come to the stage of acknowledgement. It means the completion of research and arrival at the stage of gratitude-making. Words cannot express how indebted I am to my supervisor for the supervision he provided to me. I thank him for all his time and guidance. I also thank all those people who directly or indirectly helped me to complete this thesis. I am responsible for all the errors in the thesis.

In the example above the *reflective move* is 'Well! Everybody who carried out research knew what it takes to come to the stage of acknowledgement. It means the completion of research and arrival at the stage of gratitude-making.' The *thanking move* is 'Words cannot express how indebted I am to my supervisor for the supervision he provided to me. I thank him for all his time and guidance. I also thank all those people who directly or indirectly helped me to complete this thesis.' And the *announcing move* is 'I am responsible for all the errors in the thesis.'

Thus, this example illustrates the usual three stages of the acknowledgement. However, the indispensable stage is the stage of *thanking* without which the acknowledgement just does not get materialized.

Abstract

This is one of the most important components of thesis. It carries the gist of the research. It presents the findings and contributions of the research concisely. It presents the description of the research problem, the researcher's method of solving it and the results. It gives information about chapters and what each chapter of the thesis contains. Abstract must have the heading as 'Abstract' on top of the page. At the most 'Abstract' can be 5 per cent of the total length of the thesis. In some universities, the examiners are first sent the 'Abstract' of the thesis, after going through it, the examiners either give consent to evaluate the thesis or reject it. When they consent to evaluate the thesis then it is sent to them. Some supervisors suggest giving the resume along with the 'Abstract' even in the thesis. In such cases the Abstract begins with a paragraph stating the researcher's complete name with the family name first, then the abbreviation of the degree, after that the name of the university which is granting the degree; next title of the thesis, and finally the name of the supervisor. Usually Abstract does not contain references.

There is one important linguistic aspect connected with the writing of Abstract. That is, which verb tense must be used to write Abstract? Cooley and Lewkowicz (2003, in Paltridge and Starfield, p. 159) say that there are two ways that the student may view their Abstract: as a summary of their thesis or dissertation or as a summary of the research that was carried out. The first of these will typically use the *present simple* tense (this thesis examines...). The second will typically use the *past simple* tense (The study revealed that...) and the *present perfect* tense (Previous research has revealed...).

Table of Content

The Content Page of the thesis guides the readers to see the outline of the systematic presentation of the research. Table of Content page must present the detail contents of the thesis in respect of chapters, chapters' heading, sub-headings, bibliography, index, and appendixes information with page numbers. Thus, two essential elements of Content Page are the content headings and the page number. The Content Page is paginated with roman numerals. The Content Page of thesis or dissertation is not different from any published work. However, the element of presenting the heading and sub-headings in details for the ease of the examiner and the readers is what mostly separates Content Page in thesis from the Content Page in book.

Sample Table of Content

Box 5.4

Source: Shirisha Kumari, B. (2008) *A Phonetic Study of English Spoken by Software Engineers,* Hyderabad: EFLU, Unpublished MPhil Thesis.

List of Tables

The List of Tables page is optional. Some theses contain them some do not. If the tables are found in the thesis then they must contain exactly the same numbers and labels or captions as they appear in the text of the thesis and the appendixes. And the page numbers on which they appear. List of Tables page must have the heading: 'List of Tables'.

List of Figures

The List of Figures page is also optional. Some theses contain them some do not. If the figures are found in the thesis then they must contain exactly the same numbers and labels or captions as they appear in the text of the thesis and the appendixes; and the page numbers on which they appear. List of Figures page must have the heading: 'List of Figures'.

List of Symbols

List of Symbols, abbreviations, nomenclature, and acronyms must be presented in the thesis if it carries them. The page should begin with appropriate heading. Proper explanation, definition of each entry in them must be provided. The terminological distinctions that mark the work must be appropriately highlighted.

Body of the Thesis

The real research is presented in the body of the thesis. It can be divided into four to ten chapters according to the subject and the nature of the research. If the thesis is presented in the traditional monograph format then it mostly carries, introduction, literature survey, the methodology or procedure chapter, the main chapter that discusses the research problems and findings and finally the conclusion chapter. However, a researcher may require having up to 10 chapters in his research to present his views logically and systematically. Thus, the thesis layout in science and language research may be (1) Introduction, (2) Background Study, (3) Review of Literature, (4) Procedure, (5) Data Analysis, (6) Design, (7) Results/Findings, (8) Implementation of Findings, (9) Critical Assessment of the Own Work, (10) Conclusion, etc. However, in literary research it may be as simple as

(1) Introduction, (2) Review of Literature, (3) Methodology, (4) Study of the Work, and (5) Conclusions.

In Sciences, nowadays the integrated article type of format is also used for thesis; where the thesis is constructed around chapters that carry related problems. These chapters may include published, unpublished and submitted articles. Every chapter must begin on a new page. The chapter number is given followed by the title of the chapter.

Introductory Chapter

Introduction is of paramount importance. The researcher objectifies his research and its aims in the introductory chapter. It is a chapter where the researcher proclaims the necessity of his research. Swales and Feak (1994, qtd. in Paltridge 82) argue that it is in the introduction that the writer makes claims for the centrality or significance of the research in question and begins to outline the overall argument of the thesis. They present a table that shows typical moves in thesis introduction in the following manner:

Move 1: *Establishing a research territory*

(a) by showing that the general research area is important, central, interesting, problematic or relevant in some way (optional)

(b) by providing background information about the topic (optional)

(c) by introducing and reviewing items of previous research in the area (obligatory)

Move 2: *Establishing a niche*

(a) by indicating a gap in the previous research, raising a question about it, or extending previous knowledge in some way (obligatory)

(b) by identifying a problem or need (optional)

Move 3: *Occupying the niche*

(a) by outlining purposes/aims, or stating the nature of the present research or research questions/hypothesis (obligatory)

(b) by announcing principal findings/stating value of research (optional)

(c) by indicating the structure of the thesis and providing mini-synopsis (previews) of each subsequent chapter (obligatory)

(d) by outlining the theoretical position (optional)

(e) by describing the methods used in the study (optional)

(Swales, Feak 1994: 175, and Bunton 2002: 67, qtd. in *Paltridge* 2007: 83)

Though the arguments presented above are labelled in terms of moves, the importance of introductory chapter cannot be lessened in any way. It provides background information, states the importance of research, establishes the indispensable nature of the research, etc. However, the organisation of introduction may differ from thesis to thesis and subject to subject. For instance review of literature may be included in some theses in the introductory chapter, in others they may be slotted as a separate chapter. In some theses in the introduction itself research question, problem, and hypothesis may be presented, yet in others they may form the central part of the chapter on procedure/design/methodology of research. Thus, a researcher is free to organise his introduction as he wishes. The important thing is to establish in the introduction the centrality and importance of his research.

A Sample of the Content of Introductory Chapter from a PhD Thesis:

Box 5.5

Chapter 1: Public Speaking

1.0 Definition

1.1 Types of Public Speaking

1.1.1. Informative

1.1.2. Persuasive

1.1.3. Entertaining

1.2. The Basic Factors of Public Speaking Situation

1.2.1. The Speaker

1.2.1.1. Invention

1.2.1.2. Arrangement
1.2.1.3. Style
1.2.1.4. Memory
1.2.1.5. Delivery
1.2.1.5.1. Impromptu
1.2.1.5.2. Extemporaneous
1.2.1.5.3. From Memory
1.2.1.5.4. From Manuscript
1.2.1.5.5. From Notes
1.2.2. The Speech
1.2.2.1. Introduction
1.2.2.2. Body
1.2.2.3. Conclusion
1.2.3. Audience
1.2.4. Occasion
1.2.5. Time and Place
1.3. The Formats of Public Speaking
1.3.1. Monologue
1.3.2. Lecture
1.3.3. The Dialogue
1.3.4. Discussion
1.3.5 Debate
1.3.6. Storytelling
1.3.7. Seminar
1.3.8. Radio and Television Speaking
1.4. The Fields of Public Speaking
1.4.1. Academic
1.4.1.1. Technical
1.4.1.2. Non-Technical
1.4.2. Non-Academic
1.5. Public Speaking in English in India

Source: Quadri, Syed Mohammed Haseebuddin (2003) *Intonation and Rhythm in Public Speaking in English in India: A Computer-Assisted Case Study*. Hyderabad: Osmania University, Unpublished PhD Thesis.

Methodology Chapter

About the location of methodology section in the thesis Paltridge (2007: 115-16) observes, 'It is typically a separate chapter preceding the Results chapter in the thesis by compilation.... In topic based thesis (more typical in the social sciences or humanities), there may not be a separate chapter with the title methodology or chapter may have a more metaphorical title or there may be no methodology component at all.'

The absence of methodology section has been discussed in the initial chapters of this book. My suggestion to all the research scholars of humanities is to include a chapter on methodology in their research which shall present the journey of their research and the perspective in the light of which they carried out their research. It does not matter what title they use for it, but methodology section suggests the systematic effort the researcher has put in carrying out his research.

According to Paltridge (2007: 118-19), 'Methodology refers to the theoretical paradigm or framework in which the student is working; to the stance he or she is taking as a researcher (e.g. choosing a quantitative or qualitative paradigm) and the argument that is built in the text to justify these assumptions, theoretical frameworks and/or approaches as well as the choice of research question or hypothesis. The methodology develops an explanation as to why the research method(s) under discussion have been chosen. The section will probably require a restatement of research aims/questions and involve explaining to the reader how the chosen research method(s) will help answer the research questions.'

In other words, methodology chapter reports the procedures used, the tools adopted, and the perspective brought to the study to carry out the research. In the thesis this chapter claims how the researcher used his data to arrive at the conclusions. Some research theses, particularly the language theses, carry the aims and objectives in the methodology chapter and it is numbered mostly as chapter two, provided the survey or review of literature finds its place in chapter one. However, the significance of this chapter lies in the fact that the researcher reveals in it the soundness and logic of his research's means, resources, and systematicity of his efforts that yielded the results worth considering contribution to knowledge.

A Sample of the Content of Methodology Chapter

Box 5.6

Chapter 2 Aim and Procedure

Part I

2.0 Aim
2.1 Commutation Test
2.2 Data
2.3 Set of Words
2.4 Informants
2.5 Recording
2.6 Analysis, Computer
2.6.1 Software Package Used for Analysis
2.6.2 Transferring of the recorded Data and Analysis
2.6.3 Module Used for Analysis
2.6.4 Averaging Informants
2.6.5 Vowel Plotting and Vowel Charts
2.6.6 Charts for Pure Vowels
2.6.7 Charts for Diphthongs
2.7 Superimposition of the Traditional Articulatory Vowel Diagrams on Acoustic Charts
2.8 RP Vowel Plotting and Vowel Charts

Part II

2.9 Acoustics and Articulation of Vowels
2.10 Formant 1 and Articulatory Gestures
2.11 Formant 2 and Articulatory Gestures
2.12 Adaptation of the Acoustic Charts

Source: Quadri, Syed Mohammed Haseebuddin (1997) *Urdu and English Vowels: A Comparative Study*. Hyderabad: CIEFL, Unpublished MPhil Thesis.

Analysis Findings and Results Chapter

Analysis section can be taken as the core section of the research. It may be constituted of only one chapter or spread over several chapters. It all depends upon the nature of the study, the organisation pattern adopted by the researcher, and the discipline in which the study is carried out. This chapter presents the data, its analysis, its findings and its interpretation, etc. If analysis, findings and interpretations form one part of the research then it can be named as analysis chapter, findings chapter or results chapter anything the researcher desires. However, there is a possibility that in some research particularly literary research it may have a completely different title.

A Sample of the Content of Results Chapter

Box 5.7

Data Presentation and Interpretation
4.1 Introduction
4.2 Methods of Data Analysis
4.3 The Samples
4.3.1. The Distance Learner Population
4.3.2. The Academic Counsellor Population
4.3.3. The Course Writers Population
4.4 Discussion of Responses
4.4.1 The Questionnaire to the Distance Learner
4.4.1.1. Section I: Learner Profile
4.4.1.2. Section II: Design and Presentation of Material
4.4.1.3. Section III: Process of Language Learning
4.4.1.4 Section IV: Problems of Comprehension
4.4.1.5. Section V: Course Assessment
4.4.2. The Questionnaire to the Academic Counsellors
4.4.2.1 Section I: Personal data of the Counsellors
4.4.2.2 Section II: Syllabus of the Course Material
4.4.2.3 Section III: Layout of the Course Material
4.4.2.4 Section IV: Language of the Course Material
4.4.2.5 Section V: Content of the Course Material
4.4.2.6 Section VI: Self-Check Exercises
4.4.2.7 Section VII: Methods of Teaching
4.4.2.8 Section VIII: Evaluation of the Achievement of the Learners
4.4.3 The Questionnaire to the Course Writers
4.4.3.1 Section I: Personal data of the Course Writers
4.4.3.2 Section II: Course Materials
4.5 Interpretation and Summary

Source: Shafiullah, S. Mohammed (2007) *English Language Teaching through Distance Education: A Case Study of Dr. B.R. Ambedkar Open University.* Hyderabad: MANUU, Unpublished MPhil Thesis.

About the purpose of the result section in the thesis Thomson (1993, qtd. in Paltridge 2007: 135) finds that 'prescriptive study guides may mislead students as they present Results sections as being purely 'objective' descriptions, without acknowledging that these sections inevitably contain argumentation and evaluation as well....' Results sections are never mere presentation or reporting but always involve selecting and ordering the data in a way that is designed to guide the reader to the understandings the researcher wishes the reader to come to. The writer thus, must draw out the significance of the data, highlight significant trends and comparisons, and keep indicating to the reader where in the data he or she is being led. Liking figures and tables to text and selecting which data to highlight then becomes very important as the 'argument' is built up'.

Conclusion Chapter

The role of conclusion chapter is *per se* apparent. It sums up the findings and presents the recommendations and suggestions to the readers or target readership. Its main objective is to highlight the contribution that the work has made in the field in which the investigation was carried out. Conclusion chapter may have discussion as their first part and conclusions as the second part. In some theses the conclusion chapter is entitled Discussions and Conclusion. Some theses may have conclusion and recommendations as separate chapters and others may make recommendations part of conclusion. The chapter is however titled, the objectives of conclusion chapter is the presentation of the overview of the findings of the study and the applications of the findings in the real, educational or research or social or literary or cultural or economical life situations.

A Sample of the Contents of Conclusion Chapter

Box 5.8

5.0 Conclusion
5.1 Summary of the Findings: Learner
5.2 Summary of the Findings: Counsellors
5.3 Summary of the Findings: Course Writers
5.4 Lacunae Identified
5.5 Suggestions
5.6 Limitations of the Study
5.7 Scope for Further Research

Source: Shafiullah, S. Mohammed (2007) *English Language Teaching through Distance Education: A Case Study of Dr B.R. Ambedkar Open University.* Hyderabad: MANUU, Unpublished MPhil Thesis.

Again a researcher must understand one thing that in literature and in some creative studies, the labelling of the chapter may differ. 'Conclusion' as the title of conclusion chapter may not be found; rather some metaphorical title might be used. The same may happen with other chapters, like if there is a review of literature chapter it may be called *The State of the Art*. The sample above of introductory chapter is named as *Public Speaking*. Likewise conclusion may have a separate name. The samples of the contents of different chapters given above are all from language research. In literary research, on the other hand, the tradition is to just present the titles of the chapters in the Table of Contents. The specification and break up of all the chapters into specific contents is often not found. The research may assume a greater systematicity if literary scholars present their chapters' contents also.

Bibliography or References

It is given at the end of the conclusion. Usually, References or Work-Cited List is used if the researcher wants to provide information about only those works that he cited in his thesis. Bibliography is used when the researcher wants to give information about all the texts whether quoted or not, but helped the researcher shape his understanding of the research. Some scholars give the reference list at the end of each chapter but at the end of the thesis before appendixes, the researcher is required to give a complete and consolidated list of references or bibliography (for different bibliographic and referencing styles see the part on documentation in chapter four of this book).

Appendixes

Appendixes are presented in the dissertation to demonstrate the authenticity of the research. The material which is considered as evidence of research is what appendix carries. The result or its gist is presented in the body of the thesis. However, in the Appendix section all the papers, photos, maps, interview samples, questionnaires, graphs, tables, etc. depending upon the nature of the thesis and research are included. Appendixes are mostly numbered and can be divided according to the topics etc. The title Appendix appears on the top of the page and it is always presented after the work-cited list or bibliography. Some research scholars try to present the progress of their research through appendix etc.

DRAFTS, EDITING AND PROOF-READING

Writing Drafts

Once the researcher gathers information, does the analysis, makes his findings, etc. He is required to set them down. In other words he is supposed to make the first draft of his thesis. The question is how he should begin? Should he start with chapter one and come down to chapter five of his thesis. Or should he go bottom up. It all depends upon the researcher. By the time he starts writing the first draft of his thesis, there may be few chapters whom he had already completed. All they require is grammaticality and presentation touch. However, the thesis writing works differently for different people. Some scholars after devising their outline set off writing few chapters. It has been my observation that most of the scholars write the introduction or survey chapter in the beginning itself. And shelve them for such a long time that they become completely strange texts when they look them again at the final stages of their research. Some scholars go chapter by chapter right after completion of their research. For example there is a possibility that a researcher particularly who is doing a desk research, may gather information about one chapter, drafts it, then moves on to the next chapter. This may work well for some research, but research in language has acquired undoubtedly applied features. They are experimental, action and applied. Thus, this method of drafting chapters may not work well here. In any event it all depends upon the researcher how he wishes to compose his research. It does not matter which chapter he chooses to begin. Whichever the chapter he feels comfortable with he must begin with that. When he starts writing he must develop the strategy to his writing. If he structured his chapters in headings and subheading, it becomes easy for him to write. For example an outline that provides all the components that the researcher wishes to present in his chapter must be drawn first. Their headings and subheadings must be again drawn. Once it is done then the researcher can begin with the introduction then establish some viewpoints on it and then develop points that he wishes to present.

First draft is like free and unhinged writing. It is free from grammatical or content scruples. Once it is finished, the researcher must put it away for at least a week. Then he must return to it. This period in reality distances the researcher from the familiar expressions. Hence when he takes the second reading of his draft in reality the curtains get lifted from over the mistakes, errors and blunders which have become too familiar to be detected. Thus, a week's gap may help the researcher to objectively read and make necessary correction in it. If it requires revising, it must be done. The objective must be to make the thesis crystal clear in its presentation of ideas, theories, methods and findings. The researcher must fix the slack ends. He must try to achieve, cohesion, clarity, conciseness and consistency in his writing. The logical development of content, the use of concise terminology, avoidance of colloquial expressions, superfluity of expressions, appropriate transitions from paragraph to paragraph, use of correct linking words are necessary things that the researcher must pay attention to in his second draft.

Remember, different researcher works differently. Some start writing the thesis after completing the entire research. Some may do the writing simultaneously. It does not matter, how a researcher works; whatever way he feels comfortable, he must stick to it. The important thing is that he needs to have at least two drafts of his thesis. After the completion of the first draft, he needs the gap and then picks it up to read again and redraft it. Some scholars make three to four drafts because of their obsession with precision and perfection. It is good and appreciable. But sometimes making four or five drafts of the thesis may take away the taste of research from it.

Editing

The changing of any text, document or report to improve its quality is called editing. Though the general meaning of the change here appears to be deletion, editing involves addition, correction, condensation, organization. It is an attempt to improve language, visuals and sounds of any recorded medium:

audio, video, or textual. In Research, editing is first done by the research scholar himself. In publishing a distinction is made between the author and publisher, whereas in research, the first editor is the author or writer himself. When a researcher completes his first draft, he is required to revise it either through addition or deletion. A researcher must remember that when he writes the first draft of his thesis, he must not alongside make any corrections unless they are indispensably required by the content. He should just write without paying attention to spelling, or punctuations mistakes. After the completion of the first draft he must take the revising part of it. Whether he is writing with hands or typing and storing in his word processor, the file in which he is storing must be titled as draft one. Then, after editing, it can be labelled as edited draft. Finally after making necessary corrections the draft can be called final draft, which is expected, to be error-free.

According to Green (in Bond 2007: 79-80), editing precedes proof-reading. When editing, the researcher must read each sentence critically to judge that it says what he wants it to say. Words and phrases must be in the correct order to convey the precise meaning intended, avoiding ambiguity. Paragraphs must be in logical order. Tables, charts and graphs must appear near the text to which they refer. Punctuation should be appropriate to help convey the accurate meaning. Editing is a thinking activity in which what is written is judged objectively.

According to Bush and Campbell (1995: 1) an editor is someone who improves other people's writing. However, in thesis writing, the researcher himself becomes the editor of his text. He is required to make the improvement by himself. If somebody does the editing, it is considered to be a severe violation of thesis writing by some universities. Though hardly any rule pertaining to the editing of the thesis by others than the researcher himself is found in any university, it is considered to be a moral duty of the researcher that the researcher himself does the editing, for writing in research also trains researcher to become a good editor, a good proof-reader, etc. besides a good investigator and writer.

Proof-Reading

Reading the copy of any text to detect errors and then correct them is called proof-reading. When a manuscript is typed, typographical errors somehow find their place in the typescript, through mistyping, misunderstanding the word, or misreading the words by the typist. Thus a proof-reader checks the typeset copy and marks the errors employing standard proof correction marks.

Green (in Bond 2007: 79-80) says that proof-reading involves *mechanically reading words* and not ideas. It is looking for typographical errors, misspellings, forgotten and misplaced punctuation and/or correct use of capital letters, noun and verb plurals, formatting, spacing, numbering. Proof-reading is not reading for sense, meaning or ideas; it is a reading to catch mechanical errors.

The researcher, besides himself proof-reading his thesis, must request at least two other persons to proof read it. One of the proof-readers must be an outsider to the subject, as this will help in identifying the way a layman takes the work and points out literals, typos, etc. Today mostly all Word-processors offer spell-check, grammar, and thesaurus options in their menu. However, certain spelling mistakes, for example *of-off*, *there-their*, *to-two*, *in-inn*, *through-thorough*, etc., and structural complexities can be only understood by humans. That is why, in addition to computer proof-reading, proof reading must be done by a human being.

THESIS SUBMISSION AND THESIS DEFENSE

The University/School/Department Requirements

Every university/school/department has its own rules and regulations as to the thesis submission and defense. In some universities the style books prescribed or developed by the university has to be followed in the preparation of the thesis. And consequently they also give rules and regulations about the thesis submission and defense. Some universities allow their schools to decide what type of thesis they admit and what type of thesis defense they conduct; and some schools of the universities in turn even allow their departments to have their own special ways to admit thesis and conduct thesis defense. Therefore, it is advisable for the research scholar to find out what type of thesis defense is conducted in the university where he registered for his research. Mostly supervisors help in this regard, but it is better if the student goes to the university office and finds out personally as to where he gets complete information pertaining to the procedure of thesis submission and thesis defense. Mostly universities prepare leaflet that gives complete information from the registration to the result. If it is available then the researcher has no problem but if it is prepared by the school or department, the university directs the researcher to the concerned office which would be mostly the dean's office or the head of the department's office. In some universities the information could be gathered from the Controller of the Examination or Press of the university. The candidate can approach the other way round also. In some universities the school is called Graduate School, which offers doctoral courses. In some universities instead of school the term Faculty is used. In any event whichever office provides the information the researcher must approach it and gather information pertaining to, (1) The requirements of the university for the submission of thesis. (2) Thesis submission fees. (3) The thesis defense or viva examination. (4) The Examiners' Board, as some universities allow the student through his supervisor, guide, or advisor to approach the examiners before taking the viva for if they have special questions or objections to the thesis it could be sorted out or clarified. Nevertheless, some universities strictly prohibit such practice. And in India, there is no question of approaching particularly the external examiner before the *viva voce* or thesis defense. (5) The date and time of the viva and (6) the mode of presentation, etc.

Submission Procedure

As mentioned above different universities stipulate different methods of submission. In some universities after the conducting of thesis defense, the thesis is submitted. However, in India, first the thesis is sent to the external examiners, and based on their reports the candidate is either asked to take the viva voce examination or revise the thesis. Once the candidate is asked to take the viva, he can be pretty sure that the reports are positive, otherwise he would not be asked to take the viva. However, the external reports may suggest few changes which the researcher is supposed to make and then again submit the thesis in the thesis-accepting branch of examination which is called confidential section in some universities. Thus, in India first thesis submission takes place than the viva is conducted.

One of the famous universities of India, Osmania University in its 'PhD Rules and Regulations' flier for the academic year 2006-07 and thenceforth, presents the thesis submission rules in the following manner:

> .... After the completion of his/her PhD thesis, each candidate is required to submit to the controller of Examinations, the following along with the prescribed application form:
>
> (i) Four copies of the thesis incorporating a certificate from the supervisor to the effect that the thesis is an original work of the candidate and a certificate by the candidate to the effect that the thesis either in part or full does not constitute any part of any thesis/dissertation/monograph submitted by him/her or any other person to this or any other university/institute.
>
> (ii) A demand draft drawn in favour of the Controller of Examinations for the prescribed fee.
>
> (iii) Memorandum of Marks of Pre-PhD/MPhil Examination and copy of the PG/Degree.
>
> (iv) A copy of the letter of admission/extension to the PhD course along with a proof of having satisfied all conditions, if any, stipulated at the time of admission.
>
> (v) A copy of permission letter for change of title/supervisor/topic, if any.
>
> (vi) Certification from the Head of the Department, and the Dean of the concerned faculty, that the candidate has presented the required number of seminars, he/she conducted research work in an institution recognized for the purpose by the University, and

above the leave particulars in case of part-time research scholar.

(vii) No Dues certificate from the chief warden, principal of the concerned campus college and the Librarians of the Seminar and University Library.

A thesis submitted for the adjudication shall conform to the following specifications:

(i) It must be typed on Quarto Bond/A4 size paper approximately 11 inches/27.94 cms by 9 inches/ 22.86 cms. For drawings and maps, these restrictions do not apply. Binding should conform to the norms fixed by the University Library.

(ii) A candidate has to submit 4 copies of the synopsis of the thesis to the supervisor at least three months before the actual submission of the PhD thesis.

(iii) The Supervisor of the candidate shall send within two weeks from the date of receiving the copies of the synopsis from the candidate, a panel of nine examiners, from outside the State of Andhra Pradesh (Osmania University is located in Hyderabad in the State of Andhra Pradesh in India), along with 4 copies of synopsis to the Chairperson, Board of Studies for the purpose of adjudication. The Board of Studies thereafter may add 3 more names to the panel. The Chairperson, Board of Studies, will then forward the approved panel of 12 names along with the four copies of the Synopsis for further action to the controller of Examinations within fortnight.

(iv) Out of the panel of 12 names (examiners) submitted, at least 9 shall be out of the state of A.P. and preferably, not more than one from the same institution. The panel of names is to be submitted with all particulars, like complete address, on a neatly typed sheet.

Evaluation/Adjudication

(a) Three independent Examiners/Referees appointed for the purpose by the University shall do the Evaluation/ Adjudication of the thesis.

(b) The Controller of Examinations, while communicating the appointment to the Examiner, shall send a copy of the synopsis of the thesis and seek his/her willingness to adjudicate it based on the synopsis submitted. After obtaining the assent of the examiner, a copy of the thesis will be sent with a request to submit his/her report in a prescribed format. The format consists of three parts. Part-1: A detailed evaluation, Part 2: A detailed report mentioning the strengths and weaknesses of the thesis, and Part-3: A final recommendation.

(c) A candidate needs to score a minimum of 50 per cent of the points in Part-1 to be eligible for the viva voce examination. As a final recommendation, the examiner is to state in clear/unequivocal terms whether, in his/her opinion:

  (i) The thesis can be accepted for the award of the PhD degree in its present form. OR

  (ii) The thesis be revised and submitted. OR

  (iii) The thesis is rejected.

  (iv) After all the 3 reports are received a decision is to be taken for the conduct of the *viva voce* examination before the award of the PhD degree.... [Osmania University, *Ph.D. Rules and Regulations* (For the students admitted during the Academic year 2006-07 and after) pp. 9-12]

Thesis Defense/Viva Voce Examination

Once the reports on the thesis arrive from the external examiners, the oral test is conducted to raise questions posed by the examiners or just listen to the researcher his expedition of research and its findings. This oral test is called thesis defense or dissertation defense. Another term which is very common is *viva voce*. It is a Latin term and it means 'in living voice'. This term is more self-explanatory.

Some universities allot marks or grade even for viva examination which is counted and added to the external marks or grade before the result is declared. In some universities it is just a formality, for the reports that come from external examiners decide the result of the candidate. However, some universities may not follow marks system but performance in the oral examination is considered vital before the declaration of results. And if the candidate fails to perform in the test he may be asked to take the oral viva again after few days or months. Therefore, preparation is as important for this examination as it would be for any other examination. Some universities particularly in India insist on having oral exam twice once before the submission of the thesis and again after the arrival of the reports from the external examiners. Before the submission the candidate takes the examination facing the departmental research committee or PhD research committee. This is named severally, pre-submission seminar, pre-submission viva, etc. However, the viva examination that is conducted after the arrival of the reports mostly has the panel constituted of external examiners, HoD, Supervisor/Advisor, Chairperson, Board of Studies, members of Departmental Research Committee, research scholars, etc. If the viva is open than any body can attend it; and the trend now in most of the universities in India is the open viva, where anybody can sit and pose any question pertaining to the research and its results. However, the examiners' board shall only have the authority to decide the result. They recommend that to the University Vice Chancellor/President whose office releases the announcement.

In the following is presented a sample of guidelines of the PhD viva voce examination prescribed by Osmania University, Hyderabad:

(a) The viva voce examination shall normally be conducted in the concerned University Department by a Board of Examiners, appointed by the Vice-Chancellor, and comprising the following members:

(i) Chairperson, Board of Studies (Chairperson of the Board of Examiners), (ii) Head of the Department, (iii) one of the thesis adjudicators, (iv) one of the faculty members of the department who is a recognized supervisor and working in the area related to the thesis work, (v) the supervisor of the candidate who shall be the convener.

(b) If no eligible faculty member is available in the department for inclusion in the Board of Examiners an external expert may be invited for the purpose.

(c) After the Board of Examiners is constituted for the conduct of viva voce examination, the Head of the Department shall obtain a copy of the thesis and make it available to the members of the Board. In addition, the thesis shall be displayed on the department's website.

(d) The viva voce examination is open to the students and faculty of the Department, and to the scientists in the concerned/allied subject. The chairperson, Board of Studies of the concerned Department, shall display on the notice board the date and time of the viva voce examination one week in advance.

(e) The Board of Examiners, who conduct the viva voce examination shall either recommend for the award of the PhD degree or recommend that the candidate be asked to take the viva voce a second time giving reasons thereof. The second viva voce examination shall be conducted by the same set of examiners, and not earlier than three months but not later than six months of the date of the first viva voce examination. The Dean of the concerned faculty shall participate in the second viva voce examination, and record his/her observations and send it directly to the controller of the examinations, OU.

(Osmania University, *Ph.D. Rules and Regulations* (For the students admitted during the Academic year 2006-07 and after) pp. 13-15)

The Preparation of the Thesis Defense

First of all the researcher is required to go through his thesis at least two times before he takes the viva voce examination. It is my personal experience and I have also noticed that most of us do not touch the thesis after submission. Because whenever we do so we find lots of mistakes in our research. New ideas come to our minds, new doubts get raised, new apprehensions about our work looms large on us. And more than most after three to five years of constant work we get tired also, thus we just do not like to see what we did in our thesis. We let it lie for months until we get the communication that the reports have arrived from the external examiners and we have to defend our thesis now in the viva exam. This information hurls us into the jittery world of nervousness mixed with suspicion and exhilaration. We feel happy that we are conducting the viva which means the reports are in favour, if it were not we would never be asked to take the viva exam. We get nervous because we think what if we are posed questions beyond our capacity to handle, what if the viva examiners' board or panel refuses to accept our contentions, answers, etc. and fail us in the viva, so on and so forth.

Continuous Preparation

My suggestion to all the researchers is after submission of thesis, never to shelve their own copy of thesis. It is perfectly all right if they take a break of a week or two, but after that they must read at least a 10th part of their thesis daily which shall not take more than an hour. This way, reading in one go before the viva, can be avoided. For the researchers would feel at ease with their thesis. And more than most, as they read again and again they find several mistakes which escaped them before the submission. So now they have the time to note them down and once the reports come and theses come back to the department concerned by taking permission the researchers can make necessary changes and rectification of literals, typos, etc. And if the examiners in their report also pointed out to such literals the job becomes very easy. Next this continuous reading right after submission helps the researchers to find out several more connected issues, which become an asset to them during the viva where they can offer their help to those who wish to undertake research in such areas.

Preparation of Question List

A researcher is just not required to read a thesis like a plain reader seeking information, etc. The researcher's reading of his thesis must be of critical nature. That is, every argument that the researcher presented, every finding that he made, every piece of contribution that he claimed his research has made must be scrutinized with the microscope of suspicion. He must raise doubts, questions and suspicion about his work himself. And then think of clearing the doubts, answering the questions, and effacing the suspicion. This can be easily achieved through anticipation. The researcher needs to anticipate questions and prepare answers for them. And answers must also be multiple kinds, because some may be rejected outright by the examiners. In such case if the researcher offers more than one solution or answer to the question raised by the examiner in the viva voce examination, he will certainly cut an impression of an investigator who has done his home work and who has his palm on the pulse of every problem. I remember when I prepared for my PhD viva examination I had prepared questions page by page and point by point; at the end of each chapter I had about 50 questions ready. Since my study was spread over six chapters I had prepared for about more than three hundred questions. This helped me so much that when I went to the Viva, I felt I had a complete command over my entire subject. However, to my surprise in the viva I had to just make my presentation and answer few questions. And I received lots of appreciation and suggestions as to what I should do to further my enquiry. I must have felt like this certainly because of my preparation, if I had not prepared, then the simple questions that were raised, would have unsettled me. Thus, my advice to every research scholar is to prepare, and things become cinch in viva voce.

What to Speak in the Thesis Defense?

Mostly, the panel of examiners for viva voce examination asks the researcher to speak about his research. Here, I have found plenty of researchers try to explain to the examiners whatever they did chapter-wise. This evokes ennui from the examiners and audience. The examiners and audience in reality want to listen to the contribution that the researcher made in the field that he investigated, and not any descriptive story. Thus, it is of paramount importance for every research scholar to present his findings and lay emphasis on the contributory aspect of his research in his presentation. The more time the researcher gives in his presentations to his findings, contribution and suggestions, the more he impresses the examiners and audiences. For I feel in reality viva examination is a matter of 'cutting impressions'. Because the research has been carried out, the reports have arrived and are positive, and then what more is required now? Thus it is a matter of impression. And sometimes, the external examiners in the viva, if they get impressed, may offer the researcher to take up some project with them which itself is equivalent to a great honour. As against this if the researcher begins from the scratch about his research his presentation may in first place be very lengthy and by the time he reaches to the contribution of his research he would find that he has lost the attention of most of his examiners. And rather than focusing on the contribution of the research they may note down some questions on methodological or some other aspect which the researcher may never consider worth discussing. And once the researcher answers this the discussion may broach on this aspect rather than the real findings of the research. Thus, it is always suggested to be safe and trigger discussion and interest of the examiners in the findings of the research, the researcher is required to give less time to describe the chapters, review of literature aspects of his research and more time to the findings and contribution of the research in viva voce examination. However, if the researcher feels that everything that he presented in his thesis is of contributory nature and he has devised all his chapters in a distinct and contributory way, he can go ahead with that.

How to Handle Examiners?

In the viva voce or thesis defense, examiners mostly come with a positive frame of mind. Since most of the universities' guidelines allow the examiners in the viva board to also have a copy of thesis, well in advance of the viva examination, the examiners may come prepared with a list of questions and appreciation. Mostly, their aim is to raise genuine questions or questions which disturb them. If they hold a particular theory or represent a particular school of thought and if the research is little critical of them then they raise several questions. Here, a researcher needs to be tactful and his replies must be of inclusive nature. The researcher must remember that the expert who has come to examine him is an expert in the researcher's field or related field. That is why he was invited. However, if he holds a slightly deviant view about such matter, it is the duty of the researcher to play it down and be as courteous as he can if he does not agree with the examiner. A prolong debate may result in one of the examiners switching to the role of stubborn critic. However, this rarely happens. Most of them are so far-sighted that they understand the perspective from which the research has been carried out.

QUESTIONS

1. What is thesis? Trace the origin of thesis-writing in Universities.
2. Discuss the concept of 'contribution to knowledge' in research.
3. Enumerate the contributions that your research made in the field of knowledge.
4. How many thesis models are there? Which thesis model your University offers for MPhil and PhD research?
5. Devise the thesis structure for your research and investigation.
6. If you have written even one chapter of your research, try to improve it by bringing changes in its language, structure choice of words, etc.

7. What is thesis submission? List the thesis submission requirements of your University.
8. What is thesis defence? Find out the way it is conducted in your university.

6

Research Glossary

Abstract—a summary of the research and its findings presented in skeletal form. It appears at the beginning of the thesis, report, book, technical article or any other item.

Action Research—a systematic investigation planned to give practical results capable of improving a specific aspect of practice. Action research involves the discovery and the development of knowledge through action. It is also concerned with creating science for action.

Aggregate—any group of people who share similar profession, views, benefits, etc. and not necessarily knowing one another. For example, all language teachers in the country; all boy teenagers in India, etc.

Annotated Bibliography—a short descriptive or critical evaluation of the content, scope, quality and utility for each book, article and source given in the bibliography.

Anthology—a collection of poems, articles or any literary pieces of writing compiled into a book.

Applied Research—a systematic enquiry that undertakes the solving of practical problems. It involves accessing of theories to apply them in real life situations. It is also an approach to building practical knowledge. It is designed for application purposes, not to present theories or to acquire theoretical knowledge. The ultimate objective of it is to improve the human or non-human conditions in any given field. Applied research is also carried out for commercial reasons.

Article Index—any book or source or list which provides topic-wise or author-wise articles, information of journals, magazines, newspapers, etc. arranged in alphabetical order.

Assumptions—the propositions or beliefs, axioms, postulations and notions about anything taken for granted as true without being put to test.

Basic Research—a type of research carried out to develop some theory, hypothesis, or to discover some facts unknown earlier. It is also called pure research, frontier research, fundamental research, and academic research.

Bibliography—a list of articles, books, theses, or any other works cited in a thesis or book.

Board of Studies—a body of academicians or experts who decide the programmes, syllabuses, courses to be offered in a particular department. These experts comprise the faculty of the department, academicians from outside the department and academicians from the university. The BOS meets from time to time to discuss, bring change and improve the quality of education provided in a given department. In some universities the BOS' approval is necessary before the allotment of research topic and research supervisor to any candidate.

Case Study—the use of limited samples or limited number of subjects or institutions for a specific period of time in any research. Or, when an investigation of the characteristics or traits of an individual, a system, an organization, an event, etc. is undertaken what we have in hand is a case study. Case study methods are used in almost all fields of research: Medicine, Engineering, Law, Arts and Language.

Classical Model PhD—traditional model of doctorate carried out in British, Indian and some European Universities where the students work for about two to five years and produce a big book thesis or dissertation.

Code of Practice—the statement of the university or institution pertaining to the standards expected to be followed by the students, teachers and departments during research.

Confounding Variable—a variable which can destroy the findings and results of a research.

Content Analysis—the study of content or the investigation of patterns of meanings in any given text: written or otherwise.

Data—factual information, numerical or non-numerical, used as a basis for reasoning, or discussion or analysis in any study, research, experiment or investigation towards establishing theories, finding solutions to problems, finding answers to questions or just understanding any phenomenon.

Departmental Research Committee—a committee in Indian universities that decide the matters related with research. For example, giving admissions to students in research programmes, assigning the supervisors to the students, deciding the topic, conducting the thesis pre-submission and post-submission seminars, conducting viva voce examination, granting extension for the research period to the students, etc. In some universities it is also called PhD Committee, or just Research Committee.

Dissertation—any written treatment of a subject submitted for PhD, MPhil or Masters programmes. Another term for which is thesis. Research writers use the word thesis and dissertation interchangeably.

Dissertation Committee—a set of four or five or more academics who oversee a research student in the dissertation stage of the *taught PhD model.* The committee always includes the student's *main adviser* and *minor adviser* plus other senior staff who do not work closely with the student. The committee members read the student's work at several stages, but especially carefully when the dissertation is complete, and they conduct the *dissertation defence* or *final oral examination.* (Dunleavy 268).

Draft—a preliminary written version of research; whereas the Final Draft is the edited, revised and improved version of this preliminary written version.

Editing—the improvement made in a given document through modification and alterations. The objective is to make the document lucid and understandable to the readers.

Endnotes—a system of notes where all the references, explanations and comments placed at the end of the chapters in a thesis or book, or at the end of the thesis or book. These are numerically keyed to the in-text citations.

Footnotes—a system of notes where the references, explanations or comments are placed below the text on a page in the thesis or book. Footnotes are numerically keyed to the in-text citation on the page.

Guide—another name for research supervisor mostly used in Indian universities.

Guide-ship—another term for research supervision.

Hypothesis—a tentative statement, assumption or educated conjecture about any concept, action or object which is unknown. It is also an assertion about relationship between variables.

Main adviser—another name for research supervisor. In *taught PhD model,* a faculty member who principally guides a PhD student.

Minor adviser—'a staff member who works with the research students in the *taught PhD model*, but less intensively than the main adviser. Some universities stipulate that the minor adviser comes from an area of the discipline different from that which the student's dissertation is in.' (see Dunleavy 271).

Papers Model Dissertation—a medium length thesis (of around 50,000 to 60,000 words), which normally forms the second part of the *taught PhD model.* The thesis is written as four or five journal papers, of publishable quality. It will not necessarily have the integrated form of the *big book thesis*. (Dunleavy 272).

PhD and MPhil Course Work—subjects that are taught to the research participants of MPhil and PhD programmes, before they carry out their research. The course work includes 'research methodology' to impart to students different research skills; and couple of papers in the area in which the researcher wishes to carry out his research. In some universities, course work is prescribed by the BOS irrespective of the subject in which the researcher carries out the research, and some universities allow the course work to be designed by the research supervisor and the student. Some universities in India make course work compulsory for regular research programmes.

Population—a group of individual persons or objects sharing the characteristics (and from which samples are taken), which the researcher wants to study within the context of a particular research problem.

Referral—the refusal of the thesis or dissertation by the external examiner(s) to accept it as doctoral work. The examiners send a list of faults in the thesis and impose a set of changes that ought to be made in the thesis to be submitted again for evaluation. (See Dunleavy 273).

Sampling—a part, section or item which represents the characteristics of a larger whole or group or population, studied as evidence or to gain information about the group or population.

School Board—a board supposedly upper than Board of Studies (BoS) and below the Academic Council (AC) in some university set-ups in India. The decisions that are taken in BoS are either ratified or rejected in SB and the decisions that are taken in SB are presented for ratification in AC.

Supervision—the office, the state and the process of supervising the research candidates.

Supervisor—the research teacher who oversees the work of research students and guides them towards the acquisition of their doctorates. The supervisor is required to report to the departmental research committees, Dean, BOS, and sometimes even to the academic council of the university about the progress of the research work of his research students. It is the duty of the supervisor to suggest techniques and ways (besides imparting their research students knowledge required for research) which can enhance and improve the quality of the research. The supervisor is required to check the threats of plagiarism and the other such academic evils in the work of his research candidates. It is also the duty of the supervisor to see that the work has been completed in time.

Thesis—a write-up, report or dissertation embodying the findings of an original research submitted in a university or institute to receive PhD, MPhil or Masters Degrees. The words 'thesis' and 'dissertation' are used interchangeably by the research writers.

Variable—anything that varies can be called variable. It is a quantity or characteristic that may assume any one of a set of values. For example age, gender, income, education, social status, etc. are all variables. They all have more than one value. Education can vary in terms of high education, low education, and illiteracy.

Bibliography

Ahuja, Ram (2006) *Research Methods*, Jaipur: Rawat Publications.

Almack, John C. (2006) *Research and Thesis Writing,* New Delhi: Cosmo Publications.

Altick, Richard D. (1963) *The Art of Literary Research*. New York: W.W. Norton & Company.

Andrew Harnack, Eugene Kleppinger, (c1998) *Online! A Reference Guide to using Internet Sources*. New York: St. Martin's Press.

Anson, Chris M. and Robert A. Schwegler, (2000) *The Longman Handbook for Writers and Readers*. Second edition. New York: Longman.

Ascher, Allen. (1993) *Think about Editing: A Grammar Editing Guide for ESL Writers*. Boston: Heinle & Heinle.

Atkinson, D. and Curtis A. (1998) *A Handbook for Post Graduate Researchers,* Hong Kong: Department of English, Hong Kong Polytechnic University.

Bailey, S. (2006) *Academic Writing: A Handbook for International Students*. Abingdon: Routledge.

Black, James and Champion, Dem J. (1976) *Methods and Issues in Social Research,* New York: John Wiley and Sons.

Blaikie, Norman (2000) *Designing Social Research*, Cambridge: Polity Press

Booth, W.C., Colomb, G.G. and Williams, J.M. (1995) *The Craft of Research*. Chicago: University of Chicago Press.

Brannen, Julia (2004) 'Working Qualitatively and Quantitatively', in *Qualitative Research Practice* Ed. Clive Seale et al. London: Sage, pp. 312-26.

Bunton, D. (1999) 'The use of higher level metatext in PhD theses', *English for Specific Purposes,* 18: 841-56.

Bunton, D. (2002) 'Generic moves in PhD thesis introductions', in J. Flowerdew (ed.) *Academic Discourse.* London: Longman.

Bunton, D. (2005) 'The structure of PhD conclusion chapters', *Journal of English for Academic Purposes,* 4: 207-24.

Burns, R.B. (2000) *Introduction to Research Methods* (4th ed.), London: Sage Publications.

Bush, W.D. and Charles P. Campbell (1995) *How to Edit Technical Documents.* Hyderabad: Universities Press (India) Limited.

Carol J. Amato, Corona (c2002) *The world's easiest guide to using the APA: a user-friendly manual for formatting research papers according to the American Psychological Association style guide.* 3rd ed., Calif: Stargazer Pub. Co.

The Chicago Manual of Style, Chicago: University of Chicago Press, 2003. 15th ed.

Clough, Peter and Cathy Nutbrown (2002) *A Student's Guide to Methodology*. London: Sage Publications.

Cone, J.D. and Foster, S.L. (1993) *Dissertation and Thesis: From Start to Finish.* Washington DC: American Psychological Association.

Cooley, L. and Lewkowicz, J. (2003) *Dissertation Writing in Practice: Turning Ideas into Text.* Hong Kong: Hong Kong University Press.

Cormack, Desmond F.S. (1991) *The Research Process in Nursing*, Blackwell Publishing.

Delamount, S., Atkinson, P. and Parry, O. (1997) *Supervising the PhD: A Guide to Success.* Buckingham, UK: Society for Research into Higher Education and Open University Press.

Dewey John (1910) *How We Think,* chap. vi Boston: DC Heath and Company.

Douglas Harper (2001) *Online Etymology Dictionary*, www.etymonline.com.

Dunleavy, P. (2003) *Authoring a PhD: How to plan, draft, write and finish a doctoral thesis or dissertation.* Hampshire: Palgrave Macmillan.

Einsohn, Amy (2000) *The Copyeditor's Handbook.* Berkeley and Los Angeles: University of California Press.

Finn, J.A. (2005) *Getting a PhD: An Action Plan to Help Manage your Research, your Supervisor and your Project.* London: Routledge.

Gaspar, M., Meron Shepherd, Geelong (2005) *Guide to Assignment Writing and Referencing.* Vic.: Deakin University.

Geen, R. (1994). *Human Motivation: A Psychological Approach.* University of Missouri: Wadsworth Publishing.

Gibaldi, J. (1998) *MLA Style Manual and Guide to Scholarly Publishing*, 2nd ed. New York: Modern Language Association of America.

Gibaldi, J. (2004) *MLA Handbook for Writers of Research Papers*, 6th ed., First East-West Press ed. New Delhi: East-West Press Pvt. Ltd.

Green, N. (2007) 'Getting Down to Brass Tacks: The Hard Graft of Writing' in Bond, Alan (Ed). *Your Masters Thesis: How to plan, draft, write and revise*, New Delhi: Viva Books Private Limited.

Griffin G. (ed.) (2005) *Research Methods for English Students* (Indian reprint 2007). Jaipur: Rawat Publications.

Harnack, A. & Eugene Kleppinger (c1998) *Online! A reference guide to using Internet sources.* New York: St. Martin's Press.

Hart, C. (1998) *Doing a Literature Review.* London: Sage.

Hart, C. (2005) *Doing your Master's Dissertation.* London: Sage.

Horton, Paul B. and C.L. Hunt (1984) *Sociology* (6th ed.), Anchland: McGraw Hill Book Co.

Huf, A.H. (1999) *Writing for Scholarly Publications.* Thousand Oaks, CA: *Sage.*

Hyland, K. (2004) 'Graduates gratitude: the generic structure of dissertation acknowledgements', *English for Specific Purposes,* 23: 303-24.

Jones, Robert, Patrick Bizzaro, and Cynthia Selfe (1997) *The Harcourt Brace Guide to Writing in the Disciplines.* New York: Harcourt Brace, 1997.

Kamler, B. and Thomson, P. (2006) *Helping Doctoral Students Write,* Abingdon: Routledge.

Kothari, C.R. (2007) *Research Methodology,* revised and reprinted second edition, New Delhi: New Age International Publishers.

Lamb, Sandra E. (1998) *How to Write It: A Complete Guide to Everything You'll Ever Write.* Berkeley, Calif.: Ten Speed Press.

Lane, Janet and Ellen Lange (1993) *Writing Clearly: An Editing Guide.* Boston: Heinle & Heinle.

Lanham, Richard (1992) *Revising Prose.* 3rd ed. New York: Macmillan.

Leedy, P.D. (1985) *Practical Research: Planning and Design.* Third Edition. New York: McMillan Publishing Co.

Levine, S.J. (2002) *Writing and Presenting Your Thesis or Dissertation.* Available online at:
http://www.learnerassociates.net/dissthes/#29
http://www.bath.ac.uk/e-learning/gold/glossary.html

Majumdar, P.K. (2005) *Research Methods in Social Science,* New Delhi: Viva Books Private Limited

Mauch, J.E. and Birch, J.W. (1998) *Guide to the Successful Thesis and Dissertation: A Handbook for Students and Faculty,* 4th edn. New York: Marcel Dekker.

Mitchell, J.C., 'Case and Situation Analysis' in *Sociological Review,* 1983: 31(2).

Murray, R. (2002) *How to Write a Thesis,* Buckingham, UK: Open University Press.

The Oxford Style Manual (2003) edited and compiled by Robert Ritter, Oxford: Oxford University Press.

Paltridge, B. and Sue Starfield (2007) *Thesis and Dissertation Writing in a Second Language: A handbook for Supervisors.* London: Routledge.

Phillips, E.M. and Pugh, D.S. (2005) *How to Get a PhD,* 4th edn., Buckingham, UK: Open University Press.

Platt, J. (1988) 'What can case studies do' in *Studies in Qualitative Methodology.*

Publication Manual of the American Psychological Association. Washington, DC: American Psychological Association, 2001. 5th ed.

Quadri, Syed Mohammed Haseebuddin (1997) *Urdu and English Vowels: A Comparative Study.* Hyderabad: CIEFL, Unpublished MPhil Thesis.

Quadri, Syed Mohammed Haseebuddin (2003) *Intonation and Rhythm in Public Speaking in English in India: A Computer-Assisted Case Study.* Hyderabad: Osmania University, Unpublished PhD Thesis.

Rahima Khanam (2007) *Folk and Mythical Dimensions in the Selected Plays of Girish Karnad.* Karaikudi, Tamil Nadu: Alagappa University, Unpublished MPhil Thesis.

Referencing using Vancouver Style, Academic skills, Deakin University.

Richards, I.A. (1924) *Principles of Literary Criticism.* London: Routledge & Kegan Paul.

Rosen, Leonard J. and Laurence Behrens (2000) *The Allyn and Bacon Handbook.* Fourth edition. Boston: Allyn and Bacon.

Rudestam, K.E. and Newton, R.R. (2001) *Surviving your Dissertation: A Comprehensive Guide to Content and Process.* Newbury Park, CA: Sage.

Sarantakos (1998) *Social Research* (2nd ed.), London: Macmillan Press.

Selltiz, Claire: Jahoda, Marie, Deutsch, Morton, and Cook, Stuart W. (1959) *Research Methods in Social Relations*, rev. ed. New York: Holt, Rinehart and Winston, Inc.

Shafiullah, S. Mohammed (2007) *English Language Teaching through Distance Education: A Case Study of Dr B.R. Ambedkar Open University*. Hyderabad: MANUU, Unpublished MPhil Thesis.

Shirisha Kumari, B. (2008) *A Phonetic Study of English Spoken by Software Engineers,* Hyderabad: EFLU, Unpublished MPhil Thesis.

Style Manual for Authors, Editors and Printers. Canberra: Australian Govt. Pub. Service 2002, 6th ed.

Style Manual for Authors, Editors and Printers, 2002, 6th ed., revised by Snooks & Co. Qld: John Wiley & Sons.

Swales, J.M. (2004) *Research Genres: Explorations and Applications,* Cambridge: Cambridge University Press.

Tarshis, Barry (1998) *How to Be Your Own Best Editor*. New York: Three Rivers Press.

Terman, Lewis M., *The Intelligence of School Children,* pp. 2-8, Houghton Mifflin Company.

Troyka, Lynn Quitman (2002) *Simon and Schuster Handbook for Writers*. Upper Saddle River, N.J.: Prentice Hall.

Walker, Janice R. & Todd Taylor (c1998) *The Columbia Guide to Online Style*, New York: Columbia University Press.

Woodworth, R.S. (1921) *Psychology. A Study of Mental Life*, chap. I. New York: Henry Holt and Company.

Xia Li, Medford (1996) *Electronic Styles: A Handbook for Citing Electronic Information,* 2nd ed. NJ: Information Today.

Yin, R.K. (1989) *Case Study Research: Design and Method* (revised ed.), Newbury Park, C.A.: Sage Publications.

Zikmund, William (1988) *Business Research Methods*, Chicago: The Dryden Press.

Subject Index